CALL OF DUTY® WWII

FIELD MANUAL

CALL OF DUTY®
WWII

FIELD MANUAL

by Micky Neilson

TITAN BOOKS

London

An Insight Editions Book

REGISTRATION CERTIFICATE

Ronald

(FIRST NAME)

Daniels

(LAST NAME)

19

(AGE)

5' 11"

(HEIGHT)

1925

(BORN)

Longview, TX

(PLACE OF RESIDENCE)

US GOVERNMENT

This one kind of
looks like Turner!

June 1944

My Dear Hazel,

Been thinking about you nonstop. Tomorrow's a big day. Maybe one of the biggest. The invasion we're going to be part of will change history. I can't go into details, but, by the time you get this, you'll know. The whole world will know.

The men are all excited, anxious—and yeah, scared, though most of them would never admit it. I'm lucky though; I've got some good guys in my platoon. Me and this one private, a Jewish kid named Zussman, really hit it off. You'd like him. He's from a big city, Chicago, but he's down-to-earth. This other guy, Aiello, he's a vet and ready to take on all of Berlin by himself. And then there's Stiles. He gets picked on a lot, but he's real smart. And, boy, does he have an eye for pictures. He takes some of the most amazing photos.

Our lieutenant, Turner, makes us feel like we can do anything. He gives us respect. All of us. Not like Pierson, our platoon sergeant. I swear, sometimes he's scarier than the Krauts!

But don't you worry, nothing is going to keep me down. Look in on Pa every now and again, will you? This may be my last chance to write for a little while, but you're never be far from my thoughts.

Tomorrow I'm gunna make everyone proud. You'll see. We're gonna get it done!

I love you and miss you. Stay strong.

Love, RED

CONTENTS

INTRODUCTION

The purpose of this manual is to prepare soldiers of the United States Army for what lies ahead as this war moves inevitably to the next stage. The following pages will outline uniforms, weapons old and new, and vehicles, focusing primarily on the European Theater of Operations, also known as the ETO. In addition, this manual will provide information on enemy ordnance in order to better prepare soldiers to neutralize those threats when encountered on the battlefield. Documentation contained herein represents the latest intelligence and will explore lessons learned over the past three years of war.

Numerous countries have been drawn into the current conflict, even as scars from the Great War continue to heal. This war has been and continues to be hard-fought; soldiers will be pushed to their mental and physical limits. But make no mistake: totalitarianism and fascism will give way to liberty. In the end, justice will prevail. The United States and its allies will prevail. Our victory will come not from the weapons themselves but from the troops who use them; not from the vehicles but from the specialists who operate them; not from the aircraft but from the pilots who fly them.

This war will be won by the resistance fighters who take up arms against their occupiers; it will be won by the families we have left behind, who ration food and toil in factories and spend their hard-earned money to buy war bonds. Above all, this war will be won by troops like YOU: highly motivated individuals willing to lay down your lives to ensure that America remains free.

In the end, this war will be won by all of the brave, selfless souls who answer the call of duty.

Time to take the fight to the Krauts!

TIMELINE OF MAJOR WAR EVENTS

They assume a lot of things.

January 30, 1933—The Nazi Party assumes power.

October 25, 1936—Nazi Germany and Fascist Italy sign the Rome-Berlin Axis treaty.

July 7, 1937—Japan invades China.

March 12, 1938—Germany annexes Austria.

September 1, 1939—Germany invades Poland.

September 3, 1939—France, Australia, New Zealand, India, and Great Britain declare war on Germany. The Battle of the Atlantic begins.

September 10, 1939—Canada declares war on Germany.

September 17, 1939—Soviet Union invades Poland.

November 30, 1939—Soviet Union attacks Finland.

April 9 to June 9, 1940—Germany invades and takes control of Denmark and Norway.

May 10 to June 22, 1940—Germany extends control over the Netherlands, Belgium, Luxembourg, and France.

May 10, 1940—Winston Churchill elected Prime Minister of the United Kingdom.

May 15, 1940—The Netherlands surrenders to Germany.

May 26, 1940—Evacuation of British troops from Dunkirk begins.

June 3, 1940—Germany bombs Paris. Dunkirk evacuation ends.

June 10, 1940—Italy joins the war as a member of the Axis powers.

June 14, 1940—German troops enter Paris.

This is a place?

June 15 to 16, 1940—Soviet Union takes Lithuania, Latvia, and Estonia.

June 22, 1940—France signs armistice with Germany and Italy.

June 28, 1940—Britain recognizes General Charles De Gaulle as leader of the Free French forces.

July 10, 1940—Germany begins air attacks against Great Britain. The attacks, known as the Battle of Britain, last until the end of October.

August 4 to 19, 1940—Italy occupies British Somaliland in East Africa.

September 13, 1940—Italy invades Egypt.

September 27, 1940—Germany, Italy, and Japan sign the Tripartite Pact to form the Axis Alliance.

October 7, 1940—Germany enters Romania.

October 28, 1940—Italy invades Greece.

November 20, 1940—Hungary joins Axis powers.

November 23, 1940—Romania joins Axis powers.

December 6 to 9, 1940—First large-scale Allied operation of the Western Desert Campaign in North Africa begins.

February 14, 1941—German General Erwin Rommel arrives in North Africa.

March 7, 1941—British forces arrive in Greece.

April 6, 1941—German forces invade Greece and Yugoslavia.

April 17, 1941—Yugoslavia surrenders to the German forces.

April 27, 1941—Greece surrenders to the German forces.

May 15, 1941—Allied forces begin counterattack in Egypt.

June 8, 1941—Allies invade Syria and Lebanon.

June 22, 1941—Axis powers attack the Soviet Union with over four million troops.

Weren't they on the same side at one point?

August 22, 1941—Axis siege of Leningrad begins.

October 2, 1941—The Battle of Moscow begins.

October 16, to November 20, 1941—Axis forces take Odessa, Kharkov, Sevastopol, and Rostov.

December 5, 1941—Germany abandons attack on Moscow.

Should have brought more parkas.

December 7, 1941—Forces of the Imperial Japanese Navy attacked US military facilities on the island of Oahu in the Territory of Hawaii, including the naval base at Pearl Harbor.

December 8, 1941—The United States of America and the United Kingdom declare war on the Empire of Japan.

December 16, 1941—Rommel begins retreat in North Africa. *And take your stupid hat with you!*

January 21, 1942—Rommel begins counteroffensive in North Africa.

June 4, 1942—US military forces defeat the Japanese at the Battle of Midway.

June 21, 1942—Rommel captures Tobruk.

July 9, 1942—Axis forces begin drive toward Stalingrad.

September 5, 1942—Rommel driven back in North Africa in the Battle of Alam Halfa.

September 13, 1942—The Battle of Stalingrad begins.

November 8, 1942—US invasion of North Africa begins.

I'm sure Pierson's got some stories about North Africa. Good luck gettin' him to talk though. Maybe Turner will share . . .

January 10, 1943—Soviet offensive near Stalingrad. *Get used to it.*

February 2, 1943—Germans surrender at Stalingrad.

May 7, 1943—Allies take Tunisia.

May 13, 1943—German and Italian troops surrender in North Africa.

July 9, 1943—Allied forces begin the invasion of Sicily.

July 25 to 26, 1943—Mussolini arrested. Italian Fascist government falls.

September 3, 1943—Italy capitulates to the Allies. *"We were just kidding."*

September 12, 1943—Germans rescue Mussolini.

September 23, 1943—Mussolini reestablishes Fascist government in Northern Italy.

January 4, 1944—Soviet Union advances into Poland.

May 9, 1944—Soviet Union retakes Sevastopol.

May 12, 1944—Germans surrender in the Crimea.

COMBAT DRESS IN THE EUROPEAN THEATER

As Aiello once told me: "If they're shootin' at you, they ain't friendly!"

The importance of a soldier's ability to identify both friendly and <u>nonfriendly personnel</u> cannot be overstated. On the battlefield, there can be no hesitation. Recognition of friend or foe must be swift and sure, followed by immediate action.

With the invasion of Sicily now successfully concluded, the Headquarters of the Allied Expeditionary Force now turns toward occupied France. Even with Italy's capitulation, German and some Italian forces continue to oppose Allied troops on Italian soil. United States troops must familiarize themselves with the uniforms of the Wehrmacht.

Troops from the United States may be called upon to battle alongside soldiers from the United Kingdom and Commonwealth countries and, increasingly, French Resistance fighters. Recognizing them by their appearance will be critical, as your life may very well depend on these trusted allies.

In the following pages you will find descriptions of Allied and Axis uniforms to help you distinguish friend from foe.

ALLIED FORCES
UNITED STATES FORCES

Combat uniforms for United States troops continue to evolve as battlefield experience influences design and material shortages force conservation.

This section will focus on field and combat uniforms rather than service or dress uniforms for the various branches of the US military.

There are several types of basic Army combat uniforms. The most common consists of M1937 wool trousers, a spread-collared M1937 wool shirt, and a four-button tunic, all of which are olive drab. Footwear includes either Type I or Type II russet brown, leather-soled shoes. The M1941 wool-lined field jacket will most likely be worn over this. A wool overcoat may also be worn, along with leggings, web gear, and most important, the trusty, lifesaving M1 helmet.

A recent addition to the Army soldier's uniform is the M1943 uniform, consisting of a field jacket and trousers worn over the wool uniform described above.

A Marine will wear the 1941-pattern utility uniform—a sage-green cotton herringbone twill blouse and trousers. For the helmet, some Marines prefer the M1917A1 steel helmet while others may wear the M1. The helmet may be camouflaged using either a fabric cover or netting.

Navy personnel will wear either a one-piece or two-piece herringbone twill combat uniform, depending on weather.

The United States Army Air Force's flight uniform consists of the sage-green or light olive-drab B-10 or heavier B-15 flight jacket and the A-9 flying trouser with built-in suspenders.

That stuff ITCHES like nobody's business.

Ain't that a potato?

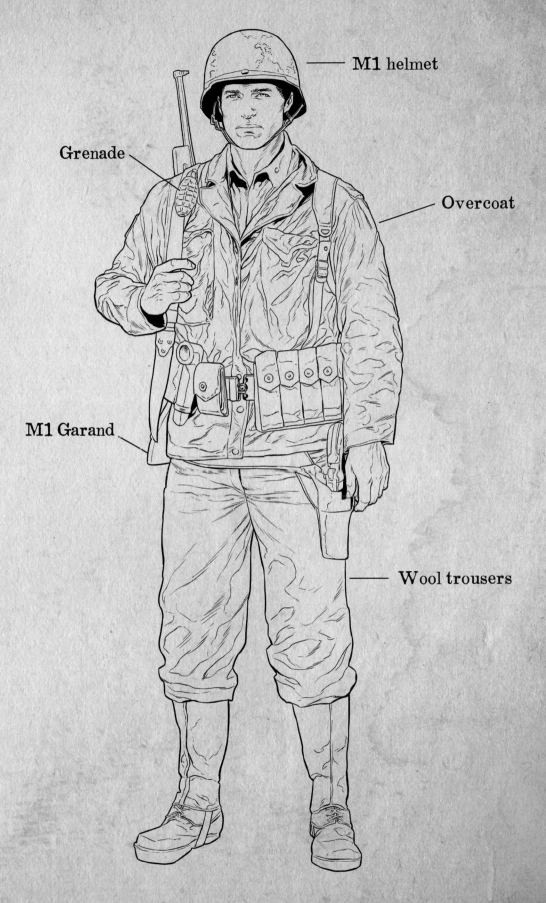

M1 helmet

Grenade

Overcoat

M1 Garand

Wool trousers

UNITED KINGDOM AND THE COMMONWEALTH

Combat uniforms for the Commonwealth armed forces are identified as "battledress" or "BDs."

Battledress, or "battledress, serge," came into use just before the war and consists of a short khaki wool-serge jacket and high-waisted, khaki wool-serge pants. The pants have a large map pocket in front close to the left knee, and there is a field-dressing pocket near the right front pocket. Ammunition boots are also worn. A jacket similar to the United Kingdom's P37 battledress blouse was adopted by the United States and named the "Ike jacket." Versions of battledress with small differences exist in many other countries of the Commonwealth, including Canada, New Zealand, Australia, and South Africa.

The Royal Air Force wears battledress in blue-gray while the Royal Navy wears it in navy blue.

The helmet will normally be a Brodie Pattern Mark II steel helmet. Webbing will also be worn, along with a MkVI gas mask bag and a gas cape.

Be on the lookout for soldiers wearing the above-mentioned uniforms, for they are your allies. Also be aware, however, that the German army came into possession of several thousand such uniforms after the invasion of France.

You shoot 'em from a boot gun.

Clever!

For catching flies

So basically "trust no one."

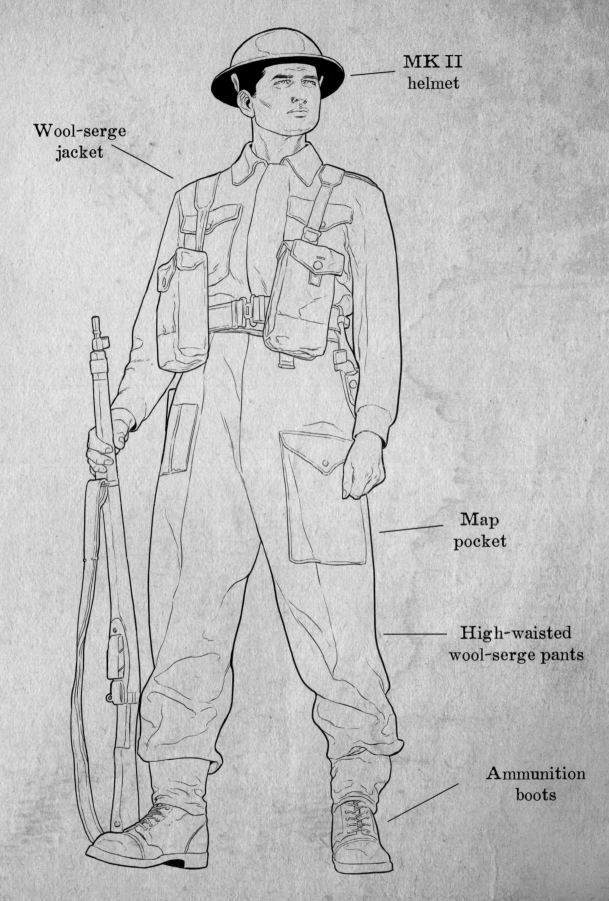

MK II
helmet

Wool-serge
jacket

Map
pocket

High-waisted
wool-serge pants

Ammunition
boots

FRENCH RESISTANCE

Throughout France, resistance forces are gaining strength. They have begun a communication network. Some have assisted in the escape of Allied soldiers trapped behind enemy lines, and many engage in guerilla warfare. Outside of urban environments, the resistance is called the maquis.

French combatants under the leadership of Charles De Gaulle participate in the multi-national coalition that contributes fighting forces to the Allied Expeditionary Force. French Resistance groups are made up of both men and women and feature members from all walks of life and many diverse backgrounds, ethnicities, and political allegiances.

Unlike fellow US troops and the allied British, French Resistance fighters may be more difficult to visually identify, as their very lives depend on *not* being recognized.

Once the Resistance has achieved superiority, and in some covert operations leading up to this, Resistance forces may be seen wearing uniforms put together using both Allied and German uniforms—US web gear over a Wehrmacht field tunic, for instance.

Maquis fighters will wear functional clothing—sweater, scarf, raincoat, boots. Urban resistance group members will wear clothing to fit in: the suit of a businessman, the blouse and skirt of a student.

The Free French have chosen to be represented by the Cross of Lorraine, in honor of the patron saint of France, Joan of Arc, and to stand as a symbol against the Nazi swastika.

French Resistance members often communicate via coded messages and carrier pigeons, as well as through BBC radio transmissions and underground networks. When operating with freedom fighters, expect identification to occur via these methods rather than relying solely on visual identification.

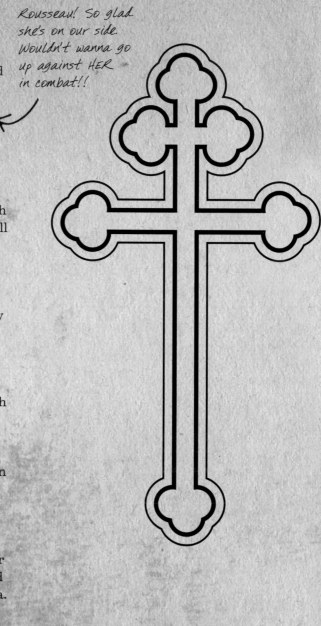

Rousseau! So glad she's on our side. Wouldn't wanna go up against HER in combat!!

Like songs and poetry. No joke!

ENEMY FORCES
GERMAN WEHRMACHT

The Heer are the German army. Variations of Heer uniforms exist, but one early model is called the *Heeres Dienstanzug Modell* 1936, or M36. The tunic, also known as a field-blouse or *Feldbluse*, is a gray green that is also known as "field gray" and is made of wool. Collar and shoulder straps are dark bottle-green on some versions. The tunic is short to accommodate being worn inside a vehicle, and the Germans used external leather Y-strap suspenders to hold up their field gear.

As opposed to a city-blouse?

Variations of the field-blouse include the M40, with field gray replacing the bottle green on the collar; the M41, with fewer buttons (four instead of five); and the M43, with pleats and scalloped flaps removed from the pockets.

Trousers are field gray, high-waisted, and straight-legged with a button fly. Wool, slate-gray variants exist, as do straight-legged versions.

Footwear consists of either jackboots or ankle boots and *gamaschen*, a type of German gaiter. Headgear will be the M35, M40, and M42 steel helmets. Soft headgear will most likely be the M43 visored field cap.

Gaiter skin boots!

For armored units or the *Panzertruppe* "tank force," the uniform consists of a short black, wool, double-breasted jacket with boots and *gamaschen*. Newer uniforms may be reed-green herringbone twill for the summer field variant. Crews and mechanics wear a one-piece denim overall.

Note that in summer months, other Wehrmacht soldiers may wear a reed-green herringbone twill field uniform in place of the wool uniform or its variants, though the design follows the M40 or M43.

LUFTWAFFE—Luftwaffe are the German air force. Their uniform is blue gray, with a single-breasted, open-collared jacket, trousers, black leather boots, and a peaked cap or M1935 steel helmet. Flight suits will most likely include a beige jumpsuit with a leather flying helmet and fur-lined boots.

KRIEGSMARINE—The German navy is known as the Kriegsmarine. Enlisted sailors wear a frock coat or a khaki summer uniform. There is also a summer white variant with a pullover jumper for enlisted men and a white service jacket for officers and chiefs. U-boat—or submarine—personnel wear a variety of clothing, but a gray all-weather smock coat is common for enlisted men and a gray-brown denim jacket is typical for officers and chiefs.

Steel helmet

Wool field-
blouse

High-waisted
trousers

Jackboots

THE WEAPONS
OF WAR

INTRODUCTION

Firepower is what wins wars. The side with the biggest, best, newest, and most weapons will hold a distinct edge over their opponent. Current technology continues to advance, sometimes so swiftly that industry struggles to keep pace. Nevertheless, experiments with automated production are changing our understanding of how to speed up and streamline manufacturing. Innovations abound, and lessons are learned and applied daily in the back-and-forth struggle for tactical advantages on the battlefield.

Sharing knowledge, ideas, successes, and failures between the Allies is critical for progress to continue. Communication is key. Most important, the Lend-Lease Act now allows the United States to provide support to America's allies through the transfer of weapons and defense materials. Our greatest successes can now directly support the growing strength of our allies in the shared struggle against fascism.

For individual combatants, familiarity with weapons old and new is of the greatest importance. This applies to both Allied and Axis armament; combat situations may call for troops to take up enemy arms, and, in such a scenario, even rudimentary knowledge of the weapon's function may mean the difference between life and death.

The following is a list of weapons, both friendly and enemy, and information about their operation, strengths, and weaknesses.

I hope lessons will be learned from the Maginot Line!

1911

As indicated by the model number, this standard-issue weapon has been the sidearm for US Armed Forces since 1911. A rugged weapon with solid stopping power, the 1911 served as the go-to pistol for our troops in WWI and maintains its preferred status today. The short recoil design makes this gun efficient, reliable, and versatile.

Not just a staple for American troops, the 1911 has come to be favored by our British allies as well. Between the Great War and now, minor changes have been made to the 1911, including a shorter trigger, arched mainspring housing, modified hammer, wider front sight, extended grip safety, and simplified grip checkering.

This new model was designated 1911A1. To distinguish between the two models, look at the gun's serial numbers: Anything with a number over 700,000 is considered a 1911A1; anything

SPECIFICATIONS	
Class	Single-action, semiautomatic pistol, .45 caliber
Action	Short recoil operation
Weight	2.44 lb (1.105 kg) empty, with magazine
Length	8.25 in (2.10 mm)
Muzzle Velocity	825 ft/s (251 m/s)

lower is a 1911. Parts between the two model types may be interchangeable. ← *"May be?"*

The 1911's fastening mechanisms are grip screws, and the tension of the recoil spring holds the weapon's parts in place, which means fieldstripping the weapon is simple and fast.

Initially one manufacturer produced the first 1911s, but wartime demand has meant that multiple manufacturers are now responsible for getting the pistol into troops' hands.

No need to sell me, I already got one.

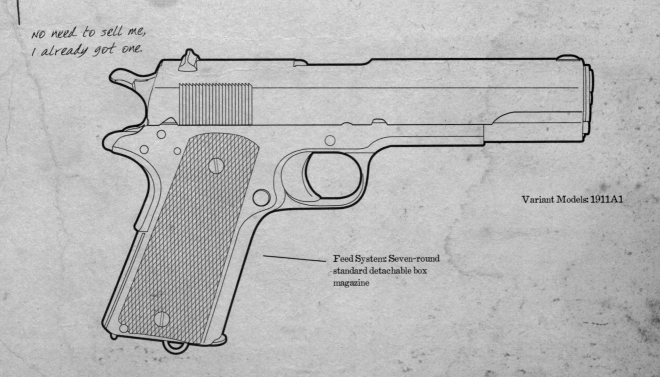

Variant Models: 1911A1

Feed System: Seven-round standard detachable box magazine

US RIFLE, CALIBER .30, M1

These .30-caliber semiautomatic rifles are currently being used by most branches of the US military. The US Rifle, Caliber .30, M1, makes full use of the latest advances in technology, resulting in a rifle with a faster rate of fire. Older bolt-action rifles simply won't be able to keep up with troops squeezing off eight rounds as fast as they can pull the trigger.

The M1 rifle makes use of an en bloc, eight-round clip. To load, insert the clip and press down with your thumb, release, and the weapon is ready to fire (note that it may be necessary to smack the operating rod with your hand to fully lock the bolt). Upon firing the last round, the clip will eject, locking the bolt open, and the M1 rifle is now ready for reloading. In battle conditions, troops are expected to fire the weapon until it is empty and to immediately reload. Loading single cartridges is *not* recommended.

As opposed to your what?

SPECIFICATIONS	
Class	Semiautomatic rifle, .30 caliber
Weight	9.5 lb (4.31 kg) to 11.6 lb (5.3 kg)
Length	43.5 in (1,100 mm)
Barrel Length	24 in (609.6 mm)
Cartridge	.30-06
Rate of Fire	40-50 rounds/min

Accessories for the M1 rifle include the M1905 and M1932 bayonets with 16-inch (406 mm) blades, the M1905E1 with a 10-inch (354 mm) blade, the M1 rifle with a 10-inch (254 mm) blade, and the M5 with a 6.75-inch (171 mm) blade. An M7 grenade launcher may also be fitted onto the end of the barrel.

yeehaw!

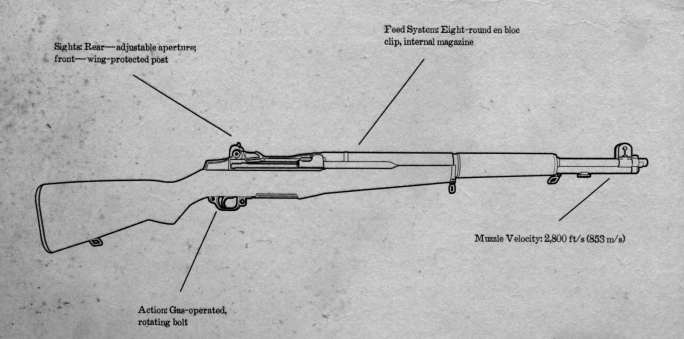

Sights: Rear—adjustable aperture; front—wing-protected post

Feed System: Eight-round en bloc clip, internal magazine

Muzzle Velocity: 2,800 ft/s (853 m/s)

Action: Gas-operated, rotating bolt

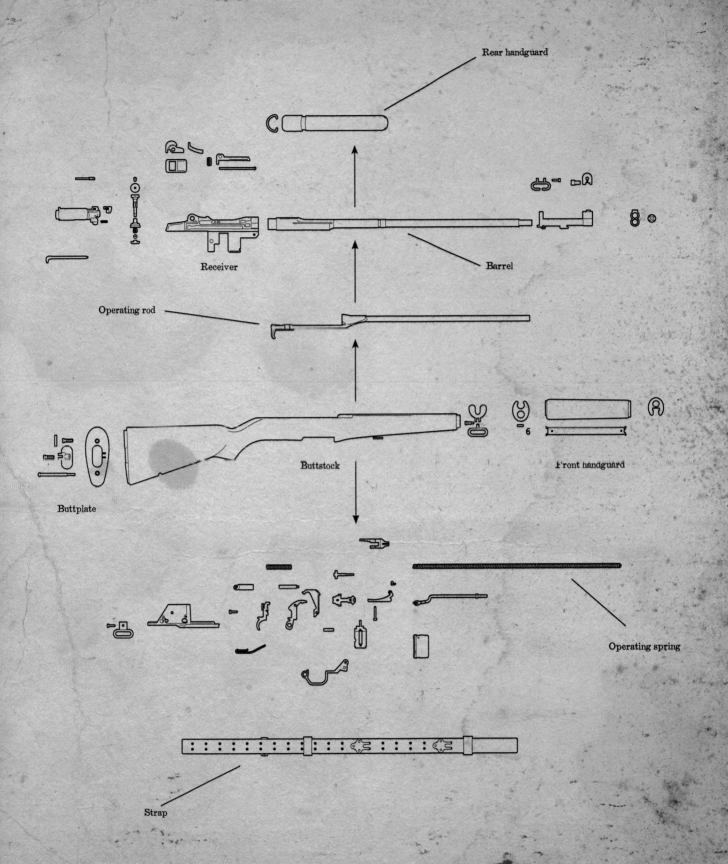

Rear handguard

Receiver

Barrel

Operating rod

Buttstock

Front handguard

Buttplate

Operating spring

Strap

M1 BAYONET

The M1 bayonet is intended for use with the M1 rifle but can also be used on the M1903 and M1903A3 rifles. As noted in the M1 rifle description, several bayonet models may be used with the weapon. What makes the M1 bayonet stand out is its shorter blade.

Conventional wisdom at the beginning of the war was that longer bayonet blades were better as this length allowed an infantryman on the ground to unseat a cavalryman on horseback.

Makes sense to me.

Therefore, surplus M1905 bayonets from the Great War were issued to soldiers for use with the M1 rifle. Additionally, bayonets made during the beginning of the current war were designed along the same guidelines, featuring a sixteen-inch blade. However, it is unlikely that our ground forces will encounter mounted cavalry on the modern battlefield, so in the example of the bayonet, the needs of the Great War are no longer practical or effective.

The cavalry is now made of tanks

As a result, the determination has been made to shorten M1 rifle bayonet blades to ten inches. To save steel, many bayonets used in the Great War have been reclaimed to have their blades cut down to ten inches. Note that cutting down the blades does not compromise strength. M1905 blades that have been cut down are designated M1905E1. One way to determine if your bayonet blade has been cut down is to look for a blood groove that extends to the tip of the blade.

It better not!

New M1 bayonets are produced with the ten-inch blade, and these are the M1 variant. The M1 handle is four inches long.

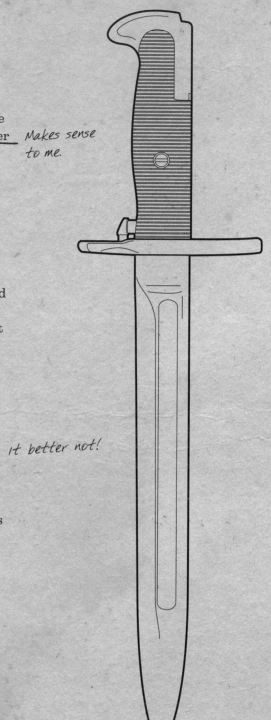

M1903

The M1903 is a magazine-fed, manually operated, bolt-action service rifle. This combat workhorse has been serving US soldiers with reliability and precision since the dawn of the century. Its successful use in the trenches of the western front during the Great War established a reputation for rugged dependability. Though the newer self-loading M1 rifle incorporates an internal magazine with a greater capacity of eight rounds, the M1 rifle has not yet been produced in sufficient numbers. The M1903—or "oh three" as it has come to be known—was the first US rifle chambered for the .30-caliber M1906 rifle cartridge. This cartridge—universally known as the "thirty-aught-six"—uses the pointed spitzer bullet.

Problems with heat-treating during the Great War resulted in brittle receivers. Improvements were made to the manufacturing process, and models with serial numbers above 800,000 were double-heat-treated. All M1903 rifles in service with our ground forces today were manufactured using enhanced heat-treating that has eliminated the previously reported structural weaknesses in the weapon's receiver.

Changes to the sighting system have resulted in the latest model of the M1903, the M1903A3. Production constraints have resulted in some M1903A3s being made with two-groove rifled

Translation: "It's old"

SPECIFICATIONS:	
Class	Magazine-fed rifle
Action	Bolt action
Weight	8.7 lb (3.94 kg)
Length	43.2 in (1,907 mm)
Barrel Length	24 in (610 mm)
Cartridge	.30-03, .30-06 Springfield
Rate of Fire	10-15 rounds/min
Effective Firing Range	1,000 yards (914 m)
Maximum Firing Range	5,500 yards (5,029 m) with .30 ball cartridge

barrels, or "war emergency" barrels. The reduction in rifling grooves in the M1903A3 will not affect accuracy.

I'll be the judge of that.

The Army has begun issuing a version of the rifle designated M1903A4 for use by snipers. It is derived from the M1903A3 rifle, but note that the A3's adjustable rear sight assembly had to be removed to make room for the base used for mounting a scope. As it is not necessary when using the scope, a front sight was eliminated from the M1903A4.

Whether in the base M1903 configuration or one of the other models of the rifle in general issue, the oh three will continue to serve as an effective combat weapon.

Check those serial numbers anyway!

Sights: M1903: Rear—Flip-up rear sight graduated to 2,700 yd (2,500 m)

Muzzle Velocity: 2,800 ft/s (854 m/s)

Blade Type: Bayonet

Feed System: Five-round stripper clip

M1941 RIFLE

The M1941 rifle is a semiautomatic, short-recoil rifle.

Originally intended by its maker as a potential replacement or alternative to the M1 rifle, the M1941 rifle has thus far seen limited use. Although thirty thousand were ordered by the government of the Netherlands, many of the rifles were never delivered due to the Japanese occupation of the Dutch East Indies in 1942. Despite setbacks in distribution, the M1941 rifle has been embraced by the Special Marine Corps Parachute and Raider Battalions.

They hug 'em.

The weapon performed admirably throughout testing, and some soldiers noted a few advantages over the M1, foremost among these being the M1941 rifle's magazine capacity. The ten-round rotary magazine is a stand-out feature that utilizes both five-round stripper clips and individual cartridges and raises the capacity to eleven rounds when an additional round is in the chamber. This is a marked difference from the M1, which uses eight-round clips exclusively and cannot be topped off with single rounds. Another unique design

That thing's weird lookin', but extra ammo's always good.

element of the M1941 rifle is that it fires from a reciprocating barrel, which has the benefit of reducing perceived recoil. A final advantage of the M1941 rifle is that its barrel is easily removed and makes the firearm compact for airborne operations.

Note that use of bayonets with M1941 rifles has been problematic due to the reciprocating barrel. One proposed solution to this is the use of a spike bayonet.

Significant numbers of M1941 rifles, along with the M1941 Light Machine Guns, have recently been provided to the Free French.

SPECIFICATIONS	
Class	Semiautomatic rifle
Action	Short recoil, rotating bolt
Weight	9.5 lb (4.31 kg)
Length	45.87 in (1,165 mm)
Barrel Length	22 in (560 mm)
Cartridge	.30-06

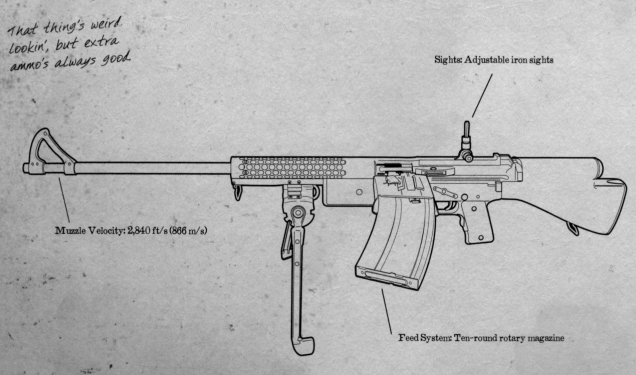

Sights: Adjustable iron sights

Muzzle Velocity: 2,840 ft/s (866 m/s)

Feed System: Ten-round rotary magazine

M1 CARBINE

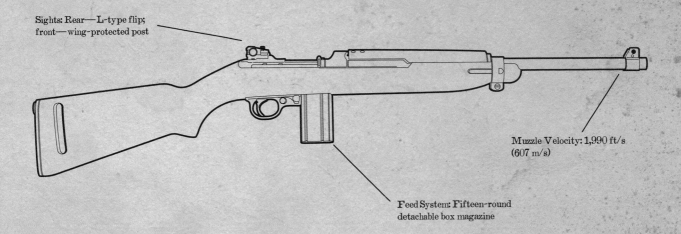

Sights: Rear—L-type flip; front—wing-protected post

Muzzle Velocity: 1,990 ft/s (607 m/s)

Feed System: Fifteen-round detachable box magazine

How about people with short arms?

The M1 Carbine is a .30-caliber, semiautomatic firearm, which means it is a long-arm firearm that features a shorter barrel compared to that of a rifle. Carrying a standard rifle like the US Rifle, Caliber .30, M1 is not always ideal. The realities of this war call for a dependable, lightweight, compact weapon, and the M1 Carbine answers that call. Support troops that would normally carry standard-issue pistols can benefit from the greater range and accuracy of the carbine. As a result, Army ground and airborne units have begun issuing the M1 Carbine as an alternative to the pistol for specialist personnel. The overall demand for the M1 Carbine has meant that several diverse US manufacturers including a typewriter manufacturer and a jukebox company have answered the challenge to produce these weapons.

Though the US Rifle, Caliber .30, M1 is three times more powerful than the Carbine, soldiers firing the M1 Carbine will have the advantage of firing fifteen rounds before needing to reload, compared to the M1 rifle's capacity of eight rounds per clip. Additional magazines for the M1 Carbine are most often stored in a belt pouch affixed to the stock.

SPECIFICATIONS	
Class	Semiautomatic carbine, .30 caliber
Action	Gas-operated (short-stroke piston), rotating bolt
Weight	5.2 lb (2.4 kg) empty, 5.8 (2.6 kg) loaded with sling
Length	35.6 in (900 mm)
Barrel Length	18 in (460 mm)
Cartridge	.30 Carbine
Rate of Fire	875 rounds/min

The M1 has a maximum range of 300 yards, but bullet drop makes the carbine most effective up to 200 yards.

A variant of the M1 Carbine, which features a folding stock, exists. It is designated the M1A1.

But will the Carbines play records, too?

Just say it has a range of 200!

SVT-40

The SVT-40 is a semiautomatic rifle currently being issued in large numbers by our Soviet allies. It is necessary for US troops to be aware of this weapon should you need to use it.

The *samozaryadnaya vintoka Tokareva, obrazets 1940 goda* ("self-loading Tokarev rifle, 1940") is gas-operated, with a short-stroke, spring-loaded piston and a tilting bolt. It is based on the earlier design of the SVT-38, which showed early design flaws. Improvements to address those issues resulted in the SVT-40. The weapon is lighter, with a folding magazine release, one-piece handguard, and cleaning rod beneath the barrel. Even with these improvements to the rifle, Russian soldiers have reported difficulties with the SVT-40 in issue service with regards to accuracy.

I got exhausted just reading that.

While familiarization with Allied and enemy weapons alike is critical to advanced individual training, in the case of the SVT-40 it is also practical. The Germans have been issuing captured SVT-40s under the designation SIG.259(r), and American troops may find themselves in possession of enemy weapons.

Though more than a million SVT-40s were manufactured in 1941, the advent of weapons like the PPSh-41 (also referenced in this manual) have led to a decrease in production.

A sniper rifle variant of the SVT-40 exists, as well as the AVT-40, a fully automatic variant of the SVT-40, with the safety doubling as a fire selector. Many problems with the AVT-40 have been reported, and most recently the Red Army determined that automatic fire mode should *not* be used as it makes the gun difficult to control and the increased strain has led to breakage.

That's like having a couch you can't sit on.

SPECIFICATIONS	
Class	Semiautomatic battle rifle
Weight	8.5 lb (3.85 kg) unloaded
Length	48.3 in (1,226 mm)
Barrel Length	24.6 in (625 mm)
Cartridge	7.62 x 54 mm
Caliber	7.62 mm
Muzzle Velocity	2,720–2,760 ft/s (830–840 m/s)
Effective Firing Range	550 yd (500 m), 1,100 yd (1,000 m) with scope

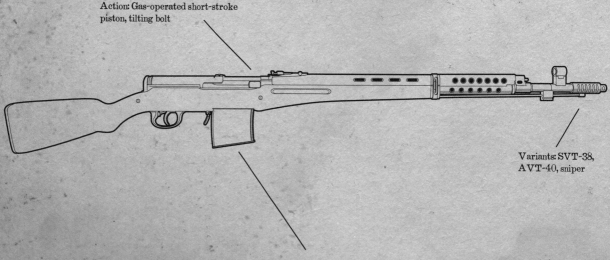

Action: Gas-operated short-stroke piston, tilting bolt

Variants: SVT-38, AVT-40, sniper

Feed System: Ten-round detachable box magazine

MP 43/MP 44

During combat conditions it may become necessary to use your opponent's weapon. It is also critical to be aware of the latest advances in weaponry being utilized by our enemies. One German combat rifle that is being encountered more and more frequently on the battlefield is the Maschinenpistole 43, or the "MP 43."

This weapon has come into use over the last year and is a selective-fire weapon with both full-automatic and semiautomatic capabilities and is capable of 550 to 600 rounds per minute. However, the MP 43 lacks both the range and power of American rifles.

Reports indicate that the MP 43 was meant to replace the enemy's Kar 98 rifle. That goal has apparently been abandoned, and the MP 43 is now seen as a weapon meant to support the Kar 98. The MP 43 evolved from the MKb 42 and has been touted by the enemy as an improvement on current submachine guns. *Sounds iffy.* The most recent variant Allies have become aware of is the MP 44. Intelligence reports indicate that the Germans are routinely making refinements to the firing systems of their combat rifles. Rest assured that the United States and its allies will continue to monitor German weapons technology.

SPECIFICATIONS	
Class	Selective fire rifle
Weight	10 lb (4.6 kg) unloaded with magazine, 11.3 lb (5.13 kg) loaded
Length	37 in (94 cm)
Barrel Length	16.5 in (42 cm)
Feed System	30-round detachable box magazine
Rate of Fire	550-600 rounds/min
Muzzle Velocity	2,247 ft/s (685 m/s)
Effective Firing Range	300 m (automatic), 600 m (semiautomatic)

I select "die!"

Action: Gas-operated, tilting bolt, full-automatic or semiautomatic

Sights: Rear—adjustable sights, V-notch; front—hooded post

Cartridge: 7.92 x 33 mm

FG 42

As the United States continues to make advances in weapons technology, so too do our adversaries.

The German FG 42 is a selective-fire rifle, or battle rifle, that has come into recent use among enemy paratroopers. Reports indicate that the weapon made its first appearance during the German operation to rescue Italian Fascist leader Benito Mussolini from captivity.

Development of the FG 42 arose from German paratroopers' need for an individual automatic weapon capable of producing a greater volume of fire for use during airborne vertical envelopment operations, which would be more efficient than retrieving submachine guns dropped on the battlefield in separate containers.

One notable feature of the FG 42 is its straight-line recoil configuration—meaning the buttstock, receiver, and barrel are in line—a design that provides greater controllability during auomatic fire. Nevertheless, intelligence indicates that automatic fire of the FG 42 causes substantial muzzle rise. Another distinct design feature is a steeply slanted, rearward-angled pistol grip on early FG 42 rifles.

By placing the magazine housing on the left side of the weapon, with the ejection port on the right, manufacturers created a more compact weapon, as the magazine well does not compete for space with the trigger mechanism. One known drawback of the side-mounted magazine is potential imbalance of the rifle. The FG 42 fires single shots from a closed bolt and engages full automatic fire from an open bolt to allow for maximum cooling.

Two distinct models of the FG 42 are known to exist, commonly referred to as "early model" and "late model" or "FG 42-1" and "FG 42-2." Primary differences implemented in the late model include a wooden buttstock, relocation of the bipod from mid-barrel to the muzzle, and alteration of the grip from angled to vertical.

While the FG 42 is an enemy weapon, its design characteristics are innovative and have already been closely examined by the US Army's Ordnance Department.

SPECIFICATIONS	
Class	Battle rifle
Weight	9.3 lb (4.2 kg)
Length	37.2 in (945 mm)
Barrel Length	19.7 in (500 mm)
Cartridge	7.92 x 57 mm
Feed System	10 or 20-round detachable box magazine
Rate of Fire	900 rounds/min
Muzzle Velocity	2,428 feet per second (740 m/s)

Pvt Stiles can talk about this stuff for hours.

Go fetch!

How many beers did they have when they came up with this thing?

Somebody finally sobered up.

Sights: Rear — iron sights, flip-up front post, and folding rear diopter sight

Effective Firing Range: 600 m

Action: Gas-operated, tilting bolt, full-automatic or semiautomatic

GREASE GUN

The M3 "Grease Gun" is a submachine gun that has recently been introduced as a supplement for the M1928A1. The earliest incarnation of the weapon was intended for use in the Great War as a trench-clearing weapon, earning it two of what would become many nicknames—"trench sweeper" and "trench broom." Before the weapon could be sent to Europe, however, the war had ended.

The submachine guns were adopted by the Navy in 1928. The Army subsequently adopted the weapon as the M1928A1 in 1938. Further design development led to the M1/M1A1 submachine guns. Some versions have also been made available to Allied nations through the Lend-Lease Act and direct sales.

The weapon created as a supplement to the M1928A1, the Grease Gun, can be manufactured quickly and inexpensively using stamped and welded sheet metal. It is lighter than the M1928A1 and uses the same .45-caliber cartridge. Additionally, the M3 can be transformed to fire 9-mm Parabellum ammunition with a conversion kit.

The gun received its name from the visual similarity it shares with the grease gun used by mechanics. Widespread distribution of the Grease Gun is expected soon.

SPECIFICATIONS	
Class	Submachine gun
Action	Blowback, open bolt
Weight	8.15 lb (3.70 kg) (empty)
Length	29.8 in (760 mm) stock extended, 22.8 in (579.1 mm) stock collapsed
Cartridge	.45 ACP (11.43 x 23 mm) 9 mm
Rate of Fire	450 rounds/min cyclic
Muzzle Velocity	920 feet per second (280 m/s)

They make it sound so simple

Time to clean up, huh?

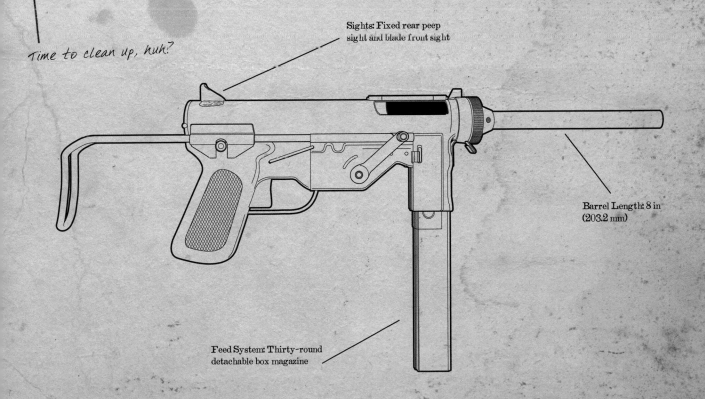

Sights: Fixed rear peep sight and blade front sight

Barrel Length: 8 in (203.2 mm)

Feed System: Thirty-round detachable box magazine

PPSH-41

The PPSh-41, sometimes called the "pe-pe-sha" or "papasha," is a submachine gun that has seen widespread use among our Soviet allies. It is a blowback-operated, selective-fire submachine gun made largely from stamped steel and can be fed by either a box or drum magazine. Recognizing the need for a dependable submachine gun, the Russians began manufacturing a weapon called the PPD-40 in 1940. Milled parts were expensive, so the Soviets soon began seeking less-expensive alternatives. Metal stamping was a new idea at the time, but a successful PPSh prototype resulted in steady production, and by 1942 factories were turning out thousands of the weapons per day. The PPSh-41 uses fewer parts than the PPD-40 and is relatively easy to manufacture.

Nope

And it's always HUNGRY

While the PPSh-41 is common among Russian soldiers, a number of these weapons are being found in the hands of the enemy. The Germans have captured and issued unconverted versions of this weapon as the MP.717(r). These weapons use 7.63.25-mm ammunition that can be fed into the weapon without any conversion in place of Soviet 7.62 x 25–mm Tokarev rounds. Additionally, the Germans have also modified the weapon to use the standard German submachine gun 9-mm cartridge. *Sneaky*

SPECIFICATIONS

Class	Selective-fire submachine gun
Action	Blowback, open bolt
Weight	8.0 lb (3.63 kg) without magazine
Length	33.2 in (843 mm)
Barrel Length	10.6 in (269 mm)
Cartridge	7.62 x 25 mm
Muzzle Velocity	1,600.6 ft/s (488 m/s)
Effective Firing Range	125-150 m
Maximum Firing Range	200-250 m

Two drum magazines are standard issue for all PPSh-41s. If you find it necessary to use the PPSh-41, be aware that the drums, even those issued to other PPSh-41s, are not interchangeable, and using the incorrect combination can result in feed failure. More dependable box magazines are now also in use. When firing the PPSh-41, the operator must hold the weapon behind the drum magazine or by the bottom of the drum magazine with the supporting hand, because the weapon has no forearm or forward grip.

The PPSh-41 is by all accounts efficient and durable, and features a rate of fire higher than almost any other submachine gun currently in use. *Yeah, but can it make me a sandwich?*

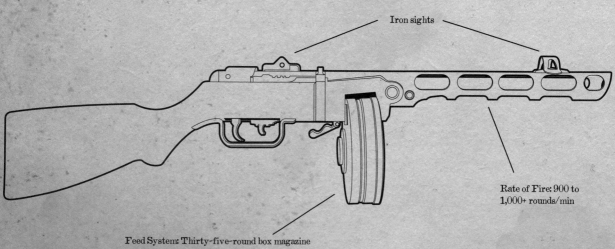

Iron sights

Rate of Fire: 900 to 1,000+ rounds/min

Feed System: Thirty-five-round box magazine or seventy-one-round drum magazine

MP 28

The MP 28 is a German submachine gun. It is a modification of the famous MP 18, first introduced by Germany in the Great War. The MP 18 quickly became renowned for its basic design, effectiveness in short-range fighting, and overall reliability. However, the MP 18's one significant shortcoming was its thirty-two-round "snail drum" magazine, which was notorious for not being reliable. The MP 28 was created with a straight detachable box, which resulted in a considerable increase in reliability.

The MP 18 and numerous other submachine guns have been used extensively in the intervening years between the Great War and the current conflict.

While the MP 18 and the MP 28/1 are only capable of delivering automatic fire, the MP 28/2 incorporates fire control components that provide both semiautomatic and automatic fire. One additional difference between the MP 28 and its predecessor are its modified sights. The MP 28 has not only seen widespread use within the Wehrmacht but has been exported to other countries as well.

Should conditions necessitate your use of either the MP 28 or the MP 18, note that for both weapons the magazine is inserted from the left side. This allows for the guns to be easily loaded while in the prone position.

During recent years, the United Kingdom's military has produced an unlicensed copy of

SPECIFICATIONS	
Class	Submachine gun
Action	Open-bolt blowback
Weight	9.2 lb (4.18 kg)
Length	2.8 in (832 mm)
Barrel Length	7.9 in (200 mm)
Rate of Fire	600 rounds/min
Muzzle Velocity	1,247 feet per second (380 m/s)

the MP 28 that has been given the designation Lanchester submachine gun. The decision to copy the enemy's weapon was made in the aftermath of the Dunkirk evacuation, when time for research and development of a new weapon to fill the submachine gun role was sorely lacking.

The Lanchester is a sturdy, well-made weapon, featuring a wooden buttstock and a direct blowback operating mechanism, a lug for mounting the Pattern 1907 bayonet, and a solid brass magazine housing.

The weapon fires 9-mm Parabellum ammunition from a fifty-round magazine, and is also made to use the thirty-two-round STEN (referenced elsewhere in this manual) magazine. A specialized tool is used for magazine loading.

Famous? Never heard of it.

Crowley called 'em the "Bentley" of submachine guns.

A bobby pin.

In case you're lyin' down on the job

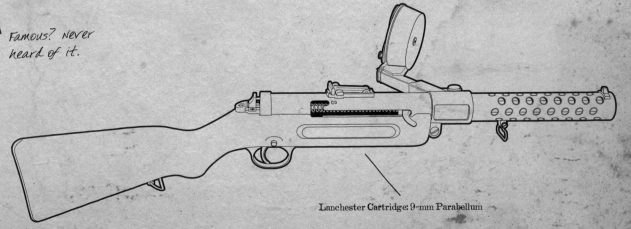

Lanchester Cartridge: 9-mm Parabellum

STEN

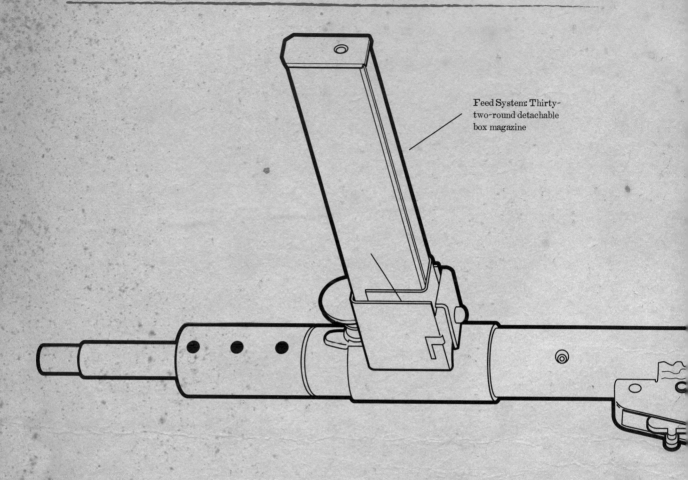

Feed System: Thirty-two-round detachable box magazine

The STEN is a blowback-operated submachine gun widely used by our allies. The weapon was designed by Reginal V. Shepherd and Harorld Turpin, and it was produced at the Royal Small Arms Factory at Enfield. The last initials of the designers and the "EN" from Enfield were combined to make the acronym STEN.

Prior to the United States' entry in the war, it supplied submachine guns to Britain. Following the evacuation of Dunkirk, many weapons were lost. After the United States entered the conflict as a declared combatant, the demand for submachine guns quickly outpaced production capacity. To resolve this shortfall, Enfield was tasked with developing a solution.

The STEN is similar in design to the British Lanchester (which was based on the German MP 28—both are referenced elsewhere in this manual), and magazines between the two weapons are interchangeable. The STEN's basic design is efficient and its look is unique, though a number of the weapon's reliability issues are a result of a flaw in the magazine design.

In the event that you are called upon to fire a STEN, if jamming occurs, it will be necessary to clear the weapon. To do so, remove the

Can't argue with that logic.

SPECIFICATIONS

Class	Automatic submachine gun
Weight	7.1 lb (3.2 kg) (Mk II)
Length	30 in (760 mm)
Barrel Length	7.7 in (196 mm)
Cartridge	9-mm Parabellum
Rate of Fire	500-600 rounds/min
Muzzle Velocity	1,198 ft/s (365 m/s)
Effective Firing Range	100 m
Variants	Mk 1, II, IIS, III, IV

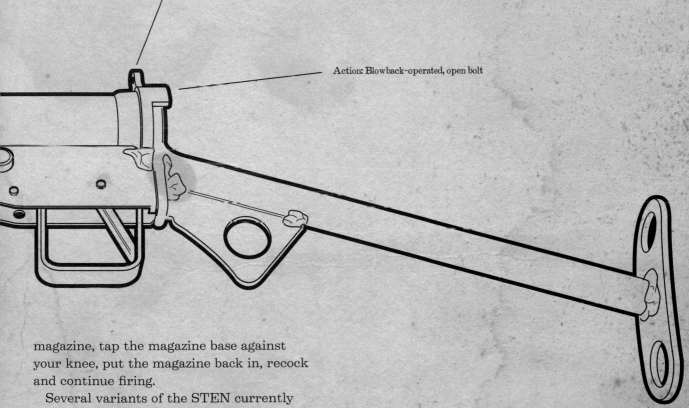

Sights: Fixed rear peep sight, post front

Action: Blowback-operated, open bolt

magazine, tap the magazine base against your knee, put the magazine back in, recock and continue firing.

Several variants of the STEN currently exist. The most abundant of these is the Mark II, which features a removable barrel and a modification that allows the weapon to be laid on its side. Foreign-built variants exist as well, most notably a Polish version built in underground workshops. Due to the fact that the STEN is inexpensive and relatively easy to make, it is favored by resistance and commando units.

MG 15

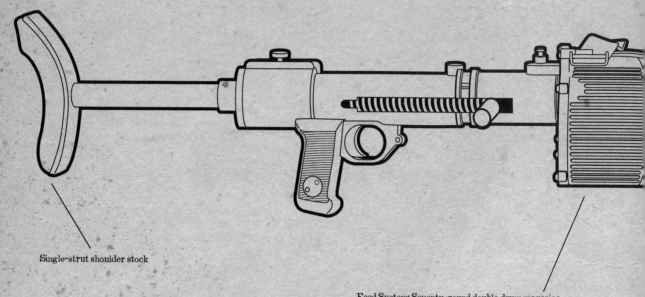

Single-strut shoulder stock

Feed System: Seventy-round double drum magazine

The Krauts are carryin' airplane guns now? What next?

SPECIFICATIONS	
Class	Machine gun
Action	Recoil
Weight	27 lb (12.4 kg) while loaded
Length	42.4 in (1,078 mm)
Barrel Length	27 in (690 mm)
Cartridge	7.92 x 57 mm
Rate of Fire	1,000-1,050 rounds/min
Muzzle Velocity	2,480 ft/s (755 m/s)

Knowledge of enemy weaponry may prove critical in battlefield conditions. The German MG or *Maschinengewehr* (machine gun) 15 is a 7.92-mm machine gun originally designed and utilized as a defensive weapon in combat aircraft. Over the past several months, the MG 15 has been modified for use with ground units as it has been replaced by belt-fed machine guns such as the MG 81.

Following the Great War, machine gun manufacturing in Germany was prohibited

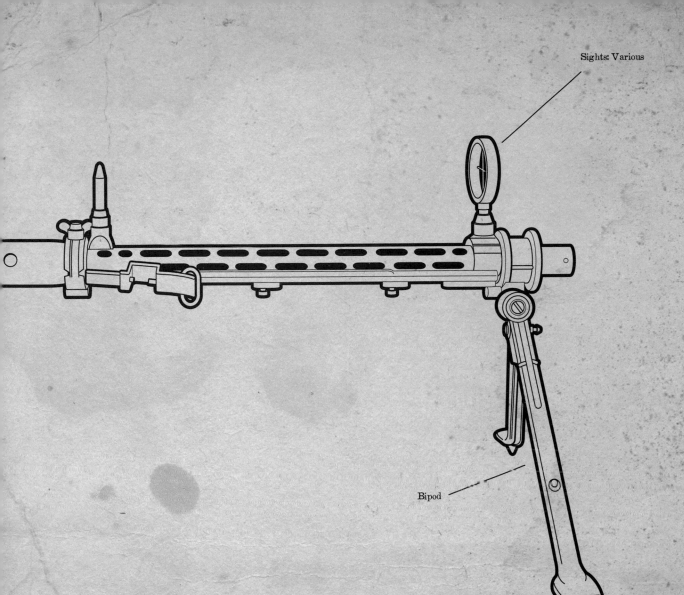

Sights: Various

Bipod

under the Treaty of Versailles. By licensing weapons designs to companies outside its borders, Germany was able to work around the treaty and put its locally developed MG 30 machine gun into production. The MG 30 was later modified to create the lighter MG 15.

In its original role, the MG 15 was used in various defensive positions in Luftwaffe aircraft, where the weapon would be used by aerial gunners to engage enemy aircraft. It utilizes a modular design that allows for

components to be quickly swapped out and is fed via dual drum magazines, also known as a "saddle drum."

To prepare the MG 15 for a ground-support role, additions include a single-strut shoulder stock at the end of the receiver, a bipod, modified sights, and a carrying handle. Though the weapon is long and can be unwieldy on the battlefield, it is highly accurate.

Makes 'em easier to ride

Sounds like a pain, but I wouldn't mind shooting one.

TYPE 100

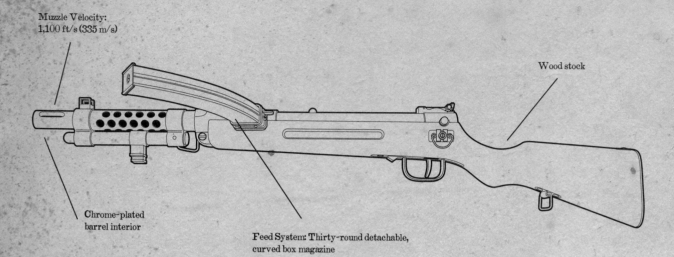

Muzzle Velocity:
1,100 ft/s (335 m/s)

Wood stock

Chrome-plated
barrel interior

Feed System: Thirty-round detachable,
curved box magazine

Though they have been relatively slow to embrace submachine gun technology, our Japanese enemies have reportedly come to see value in the weapon type, and some Imperial Japanese Army (IJA) troops have begun employing a basic submachine gun known as the Type 100. By all accounts the Japanese have rushed these weapons into production, most likely using designs derived from seized Allied submachine guns. These mass-produced weapons began appearing in 1942 during the invasion of Southern China.

Poof!

The Type 100 features a wood stock. They are automatic-only, firing an 8-mm cartridge from a thirty-round detachable box magazine, and employ an air-cooled, blowback method of operation. The barrel features six-groove, right-hand-twist rifling, has a muzzle break on some examples, and is, surprisingly for a submachine gun, bayonet ready. The barrel interior is chrome-lined to prevent corrosion, which is especially necessary in jungle conditions. Japanese paratroopers have reportedly used a version with a folding stock. Also worthy of note is that the Type 100 utilizes bipods.

US soldiers who have acquired and used a Type 100 have reported firing stoppages and imbalance due to the left-side *Happens to me after C rations.*

SPECIFICATIONS	
Class	Automatic submachine gun
Action	Blowback
Weight	8.4 lb (3.8 kg)
Length	35.0 in (890 mm)
Barrel Length	9.0 in (228 mm)
Cartridge	8 x 22 mm Nambu
Rate of Fire	450 rounds/min
Effective Firing Range	100-150 m

loading magazine. Other reports indicate that the left-tilting sights make firing awkward for left-handed operators. One advantage of the Type 100 is that it is fairly lightweight. It also requires little familiarization, though the weapon uses a relatively weak Nambu pistol round.

A recent intelligent report suggests that the Imperial Japanese Army is revising the Type 100 design. Whether or not an improved version of the Type 100 will make it to the battlefield remains to be seen.

Might as well use a slingshot.

BC-41 TRENCH KNIFE

Also makes a great can opener

Pa's knife is one of the most important items I brought with me.

Trench knives are a carry-over from the Great War, when trench fighting was common. The BC-41 is a trench knife favored by British commandos. It is also a combination of brass knuckles and dagger, purpose-built for close quarters fighting.

Early expectations held that the current conflict would see a return to trench warfare. The BC-41 was created with previous, successful trench knife designs in mind.

The BC-41 features brass knuckles—metal shaped to fit a soldier's knuckles, meant to focus the power of a punch in a smaller area and protect the fighter's hand, as the metal rings protect the knuckles and the palm grip absorbs a punch's counter force.

The BC-41's steel blade is bolted or riveted to the palm grip, which is cast in either iron or brass. Typical blade length is 5.5 inches. The knife is intended to be held with the thumb at the pommel. This is the "ice pick grip" favored by the British, which allows a soldier to punch and then stab, or punch and then backslash. It has been reported that some British soldiers removed the first loop of the grip in order to allow for trigger pulling while holding the knife.

Although trench warfare has not emerged as a central aspect of the combat experience in the current conflict as originally anticipated, the BC-41 has nevertheless proven to be an effective and versatile weapon, useful in commando operations.

Hey, smart!

MK II GRENADE & M16 SMOKE GRENADE

SPECIFICATIONS

Class	Time-fused grenade
Weight	1 lb, 5 oz (595 grams)
Length	3-5/6 in (111 mm)
Filling	TNT or EC blank fire powder
Filling Weight	2 oz
Detonation Mechanism	Percussion cap and time fuse, 5 second delay

The MK II is a fragmentation type of antipersonnel hand grenade, also known as a "frag grenade" or "pineapple" due to the raised block pattern across its surface. The deep, wide grooves allow for easier handling and provide for better fragmentation.

The fastball's a killer.

The MK II has been in use since 1918 when it replaced the flawed Mark I. It is made up of a cast-iron body with forty raised segments in five rows of eight columns. Fuses vary between M5 and M6 detonating fuses for grenades with a high-explosive TNT filler, and M10 igniting fuses for grenades with a low-explosive black powder filler. The grenade's safety pin is crimped to hold it in place. To operate the grenade, pull the pin and release the spoon. When the spoon or handle flies away, a spring drives the striker into a percussion cap, igniting the cap, which in turn ignites the fuse.

I don't care, as long as it works.

Once this is accomplished, the soldier will have four to five seconds before detonation. Note that the M10A3 fuse makes a hissing noise while burning, so the user should be aware of this when operating in close proximity of enemy troops.

Prior to entering the war, MK II fragmentation hand grenades were painted yellow to make them easy to identify. In recent months though, they have been painted olive drab to reduce visibility in combat. The high-explosive grenade should still have a yellow ring or band at the top. Low-explosive grenades will be either black or gray. Practice grenades are painted red.

The M7 rifle grenade launcher attachment can also be used to fire the MK II. One end of the launcher is affixed to the rifle while the launcher's fin assembly on the opposite end will hold the grenade in brackets prior to firing.

The M16 is a smoke grenade available in the following colors: green, purple, red, white, yellow, blue, orange, and black. Smoke grenades are used as a signaling device, to mark a target for close air support, or to provide concealment. Colors used for various operations will vary depending on unit and situation.

Stiles likes to use 'em when he's taking photos. Says it adds "atmosphere."

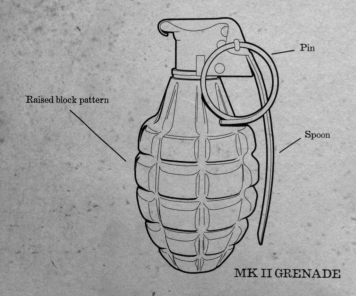

MK II GRENADE

Pin

Raised block pattern

Spoon

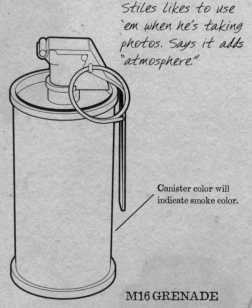

M16 GRENADE

Canister color will indicate smoke color.

Pretty much the scariest thing you can think of

S-MINE

One of the most common antipersonnel weapons in use by the Wehrmacht is the S-mine.

The mine, also known as a "Bouncing Betty" or, in German, *Schrapnellmine*, *Springmine*, or *Splittermine*, is part of a category of mines known as bounding mines: mines that are propelled into the air before detonation.

When triggered, the S-mine launches just short of three feet into the air and explodes, spraying shrapnel 360 degrees. It is most effective in open areas against unprotected personnel.

The S-mine has been used extensively since its introduction in combat during the Saar Offensive, where it inflicted heavy casualties on the French Second Army Group. The S-mine is infamous for inflicting severe wounds to the extremities and genitals. As a result, it has become one of the most feared weapons in Germany's arsenal.

The body of the mine is a roughly six-inch steel cylinder. The main fuse is housed inside a steel rod, which projects upward and is topped with a trigger or sensor. The propelling charge that launches the mine is gunpowder, while the main charge is TNT.

Most often, the trigger used is a three-pronged pressure fuse (tripwires are sometimes used as well). The enemy ordinarily will bury the mine with the prongs exposed just above the surface. The sensor will activate when a weight of fifteen pounds or greater is applied. Time between the triggering of the propellant and ignition of the main charge is four seconds.

Rumors have circulated that ignition will not occur if a soldier keeps his foot on the sensor once triggered. This is not true. The main charge will still detonate. To mitigate injury once the sensor is triggered, it is suggested that the soldier immediately drop flat, with their face to the ground.

SPECIFICATIONS	
Class	Bounding antipersonnel mine
Weight	9 lb (4.1 kg)
Diameter	102 mm
Filling	TNT
Filling Weight	6.4 oz (182 grams)

In the absence of the SCR-625 portable mine detector, the S-mine is most easily detected through the use of a bayonet or trench knife, which is used to probe slowly at a low angle. If a mine is found, specially trained combat engineers should be utilized to clear the mine.

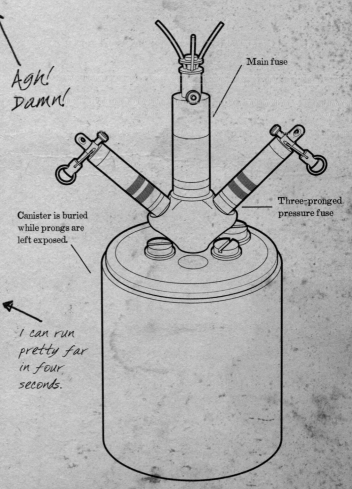

Agh! Damn!

Main fuse

Three-pronged pressure fuse

Canister is buried while prongs are left exposed.

I can run pretty far in four seconds.

FLAMETHROWER

They can still fail to light! I heard about a guy who had to light one with a cigarette!

Sounds pretty safe

Throughout history, one common fear shared by any enemy in any combat situation is a fear of fire.

Though flamethrowers have been in use since as far back as the Great War, the United States largely considered them to be ineffective. As a result, the US showed very little interest in developing flamethrowers prior to the current conflict. With the onset of the current war and effective flamethrower use by the Germans, the United States revisited its position and began developing flamethrower systems in 1940.

Early on, two experimental models were developed: The E1 consisted of a fuel storage system, compressed-gas storage system, igniter, and flame gun. It used one vertical fuel tank cylinder with an upper and lower compartment. Pressurized nitrogen in the upper compartment sent five gallons of fuel oil into the lower compartment and into the flame gun. Diesel oil, fuel oil, and gas/oil mixtures were all used as fuel. The igniter, a compressed hydrogen cylinder and battery, was affixed to the flame gun. Operators fired the gun using two triggers: one to spray fuel and one to ignite it as it left the barrel. The E1 had a range of fourteen to twenty-one yards. Many flaws were identified during testing and training with the weapon, which led to an overhauled version designated the E1R1.

The E1R1, or Experiment 1 Revision 1, separated the compressed nitrogen from the fuel reservoir. The fuel tank was composed of two large vertical fuel bottles and a third,

They make great enemy targets.

thinner tank (worn together as a backpack) for propellant. Improvements were made to the flame gun, valves, and ignition system. The weight was decreased, while the range changed to fifteen to twenty yards for fifteen to twenty seconds.

Few E1R1s were used in combat, but continued improvements led to the M1. The heavier, more damage-resistant M1 saw action in the Pacific theater starting in 1942. Despite improvements, the M1 was still prone to failures, so the Chemical Warfare Service department has continued to make refinements.

Has a real interesting smell

Recent developments have led to an entirely new flammable liquid: napalm. Napalm is a mixture of a fuel and a gelling agent that sticks to various surfaces, including skin, and burns at a steady rate. Napalm has proven to provide greater range and damage capability to portable flamethrowers. It was necessary, however, for the M1 to undergo more design changes to allow it to be an effective delivery system for napalm. Those changes have resulted in the M1A1. Perhaps the greatest advantage to be seen with the M1A1 is its increased range—now up to fifty yards.

The newest addition to the flamethrower family, entering service just last year, is the M2. The biggest change to be seen in the M2 is a cartridge-based ignition system, replacing the older battery-actuated spark system. Initial reports indicate that the new ignition system is the most reliable to date.

That's not saying much.

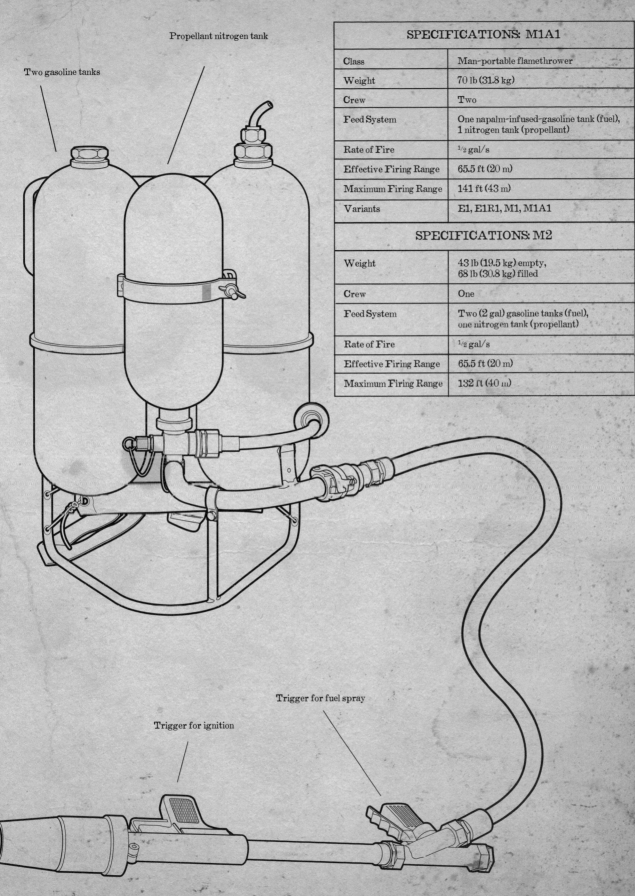

Two gasoline tanks

Propellant nitrogen tank

SPECIFICATIONS: M1A1

Class	Man-portable flamethrower
Weight	70 lb (31.8 kg)
Crew	Two
Feed System	One napalm-infused-gasoline tank (fuel), 1 nitrogen tank (propellant)
Rate of Fire	$^{1}/_{2}$ gal/s
Effective Firing Range	65.5 ft (20 m)
Maximum Firing Range	141 ft (43 m)
Variants	E1, E1R1, M1, M1A1

SPECIFICATIONS: M2

Weight	43 lb (19.5 kg) empty, 68 lb (30.8 kg) filled
Crew	One
Feed System	Two (2 gal) gasoline tanks (fuel), one nitrogen tank (propellant)
Rate of Fire	$^{1}/_{2}$ gal/s
Effective Firing Range	65.5 ft (20 m)
Maximum Firing Range	132 ft (40 m)

Trigger for fuel spray

Trigger for ignition

M1 ANTITANK ROCKET LAUNCHER

The M1 Antitank Rocket Launcher is a recoilless rocket launcher that is primarily used as an antitank weapon. It is also extremely effective against armored vehicles, gun nests, and bunkers. The weapon also shares visual similarity with a musical instrument known as a "bazooka," which has resulted in the weapon receiving a new nickname.

Like tanks?

M1 rocket launcher design dates back to the Great War, but its military acceptance came just before the end of that war, and development stalled for many years. Advancements in shaped-charge technology led to a grenade capable of penetrating armor up to 2.4 inches thick. The grenade was too heavy to be used effectively, however. What was sorely needed was some form of delivery system that would fire the grenade over a long range while also protecting the soldier. Army Ordnance Officer Edward Uhl came up with the solution after seeing a tube in a pile of junk. Following a prototype and improvements, the M1 rocket launcher entered production.

Don't they use this name for pretty much everything?

The weapon's simple design features a tube body, sights, internal power supply, shoulder support, and trigger unit. Ammunition for the rocket launcher is an M6 rocket. Operation of the launcher is also straightforward: One soldier aims, usually kneeling, with the launcher supported on his shoulder and safety on. The loader inserts a rocket into the breech, removing the arming pin and pushing until the rocket is locked in place. Coiled wire from the rocket's fin assembly is wrapped around the launcher's contact spring. The loader gives the firer the ready signal, and the weapon is ready to fire. Note: Make sure to clear your backblast area!

Improvements made to the M1 rocket launcher produced the M1A1. Changes include the addition of a heat guard and flash deflector. Most notably, however, improvements to the M6 rocket have led to the M6A1. Ignition system changes have recently led to the M6A2.

The M1A1 has proven to be extremely effective. Its size, however, does not make it ideal for airborne troops who need to carry

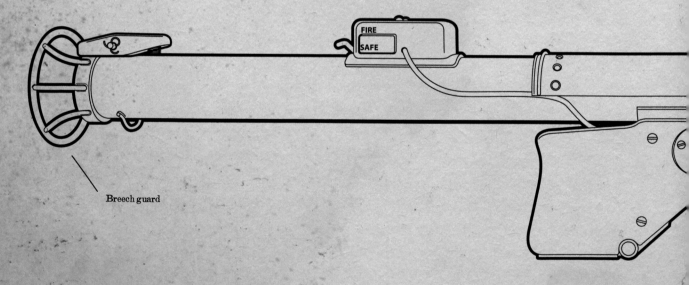

Breech guard

SPECIFICATIONS: M1	
Class	Recoilless rocket antitank weapon
Weight	13 lb (5.9 kg)
Length	54 in (137 cm)
Crew	Two, operator and loader
Caliber	2.36 in (60 mm)
Warhead	M6 or M6A2 shaped charge (3.5 lb, 1.59 kg)
Effective Firing Range	150 yards (140 m)
Maximum Firing Range	400 yards (370 m)

SPECIFICATIONS: M1A1	
Weight	12.75 lb (5.8 kg)
Crew	Two, operator and loader
Caliber	2.36 in (60 mm)
Warhead	M6A1 shaped charge (3.5 lb, 1.59 kg)
Effective Firing Range	150 yards (140 m)
Maximum Firing Range	400 yards (370 m)

the weapon in the tight spaces of an aircraft and then parachute and land with it. The M9 rocket launcher has been developed in an effort to address the airborne troopers' need. This new weapon is capable of being broken down and easily transported. Fortunately, breaking the unit into two pieces has allowed for a longer launch tube and thereby better accuracy, with a fifty-yard increase in engagement range. Though delivery of the M9 has not yet occurred, this new and improved weapon should be making their way into the hands of airborne soldiers soon.

The M1 rocket launcher has been and remains an invaluable asset, allowing a two-man team to target and neutralize fortified positions and armored vehicles alike. Advances and improvements in rocket-launcher technology, as well as the Lend-Lease Act, ensure that the United States and its allies will continue using this weapon to strike fear into the hearts of the enemy throughout the remainder of the war.

Length: 54 in (137 cm)

Stock

PANZERSCHRECK, FAUSTPATRONE, PANZERFAUST

I suppose lighting myself on fire's a bad idea too?

I thought they looked familiar . . .

The Panzerschreck is an enemy antitank weapon design based on examples of the US M1 ATRL captured in North Africa and Sicily early in the war.

Germany reverse-engineered the M1 rocket launcher to create a larger and heavier version, the Panzerschreck. Like the M1 rocket launcher, the Panzerschreck uses a tube and is shoulder-launched, but the ammunition has is now 88 mm caliber versus the M1 rocket launcher's 60 mm caliber. This larger caliber makes the weapon capable of penetrating thicker armor (100 mm), thus the name Panzerschreck, which translates to "tank's fright" or "tank's bane." The antitank launcher is also known as *Raketenpanzerbuchse*, or RPzB. RPzB 43 was the first Panzerschreck model, and it required that the user wear a poncho and gas mask to protect against backblast heat. Modifications, including a blast shield, were later made resulting in the RPzB 54.

Now you're just punching typewriter keys.

Should it be necessary for a US soldier to fire a Panzerschreck, perform the following: 1) Pull the cocking handle to the rear. 2) Load the weapon. 3) Push the lever inside the handle down to disengage the safety. 4) Fire. Upon firing, a driving rod will strike a punch generator that will complete a circuit and ignite the rocket motor.

When firing the RPzB 43, gear must be worn to protect against heat and toxic gases. Also be aware that the Panzerschreck produces a great deal of smoke and will certainly give away your position. It is not recommended to fire the Panzerschreck indoors.

The Faustpatrone ("fist cartridge") and the Panzerfaust ("armor fist" or "tank fist") are single-shot, recoilless German antitank weapons. They use a much smaller launch tube than the Panzerschreck and are meant to be used by a single person. Both weapons fire a high-explosive antitank (HEAT) warhead. The Faustpatrone is the smaller forerunner of the Panzerfaust. It weighs 7.1 pounds and fires a 4-inch diameter warhead carrying a 14-ounce shaped charge mix of TNT and tri-hexogen. Armor penetration for the Faustpatrone is 140 mm.

Development soon led to the larger Panzerfaust 30. It weighs 11.2 pounds and fires a warhead 5.5 inches in diameter. Armor penetration is 200 mm.

To fire a Panzerfaust, disengage the safety, either tuck the shaft under your arm or lay it in the crook of your arm, aim, and squeeze the lever. The tube is meant to be discarded after firing.

Married folks are outta luck.

Make up your mind!

Hey, it's not rocket science. Oh wait . . .

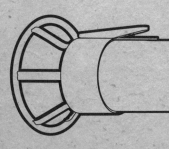

PANZERSCHRECK

SPECIFICATIONS: PANZERSCHRECK	
Class	Antitank rocket launcher
Weight	24 lb (11 kg) empty (RPzB 54)
Length	65 in (164 cm)
Caliber	88 mm
Muzzle Velocity	360 ft/s, (110 m/s) 246 mph
Effective Firing Range	150 m (RPzB 54)

SPECIFICATIONS: PANZERFAUST 30	
Class	Man-portable antitank recoilless gun
Weight	11.51 lb (5.22 kg)
Length	3 ft, 3 in (1 m)
Warhead	Shaped charge
Projectile Speed	98.43 ft/s (30 m/s)
Effective Firing Range	98.43 ft (30 m)

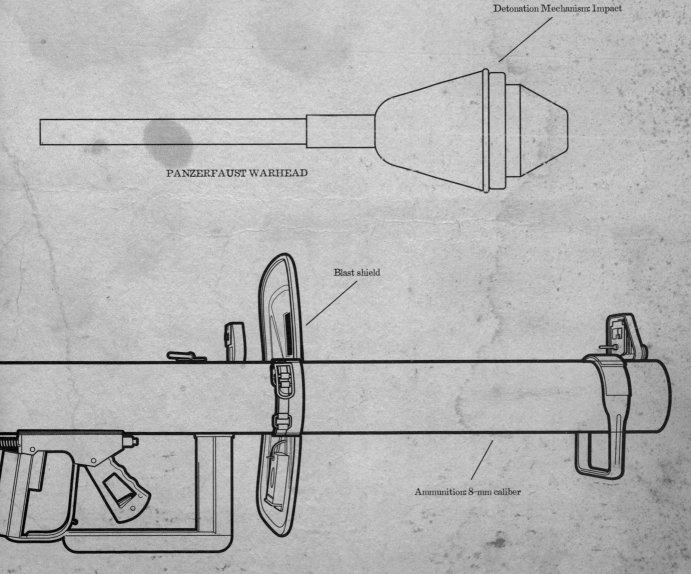

Detonation Mechanism: Impact

PANZERFAUST WARHEAD

Blast shield

Ammunition: 8-mm caliber

8.8 CM FLAK 18/36/37/41

I don't even think the Krauts understand what this means.

The 8.8 cm Flak 18/36/37/41 is a series of German guns that served in a variety of combat roles. The guns' transport carriage provided mobility and allowed for antiaircraft use and some antitank use on extremely rare occasions. The emplaced configuration of the base resulted in a stationary gun specifically for antiaircraft use.

The 88 mm (8.8 cm) gun is also sometimes called "the eighty eight" or the "88 mm Flak," where "Flak" stands for *Flugzeugabwehrkanone* or "aircraft defense cannon."

During the Great War, improvements were made to existing antiaircraft guns, resulting in higher muzzle velocities in order to reach greater altitudes. The 88-mm ammunition was used because it was considered the largest and heaviest ammo a soldier could carry. Under the terms of the Versailles Treaty that governed the post-war period, Germany was banned from developing certain weapons, but by using foreign companies, further improvements to existing weapons were made. The prototype model Flak 18 was given the "18" designation to fool Versaille Treaty monitors into thinking the new gun was a copy of an older 1918 model.

The Flak 18 fires high-explosive, armor-piercing, and high-explosive antitank

Look up the MG 15 to see how well THAT worked.

ammunition at a rate of fifteen to twenty rounds a minute, and depending on circumstances, it can be operated with a six- to eleven-man crew. After flaws in the Flak 18 were identified, upgrades were implemented: In the Flak 36, a multisection barrel was introduced that allowed for faster barrel changing. Also, an armored shield that could be retrofitted to Flak 18s was commonly used for the gunner's protection.

A battery of four Flak 36s was capable of coordinated fire with the use of targeting indicators connected to a central controller. Upgrades to Flak 36 instrumentation resulted in the Flak 37. The Flak 41 incorporated a longer cartridge and longer barrel that yielded significantly higher muzzle velocity, while reloading improvements increased the rate of fire to twenty to twenty-five rounds per minute. The Flak 41 has experienced serious performance issues, however, which have limited the gun's use outside of Germany.

The 88 mm gun series has proven to be a reliable, widely used weapon that has earned the fear and respect of many Allied soldiers.

This thing sounds pretty nasty.

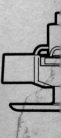

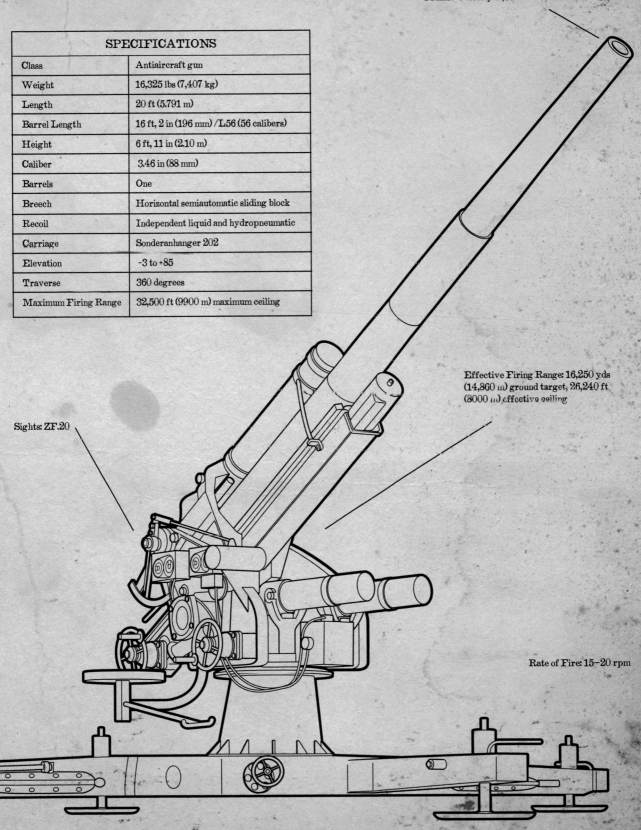

SPECIFICATIONS

Class	Antiaircraft gun
Weight	16,325 lbs (7,407 kg)
Length	20 ft (5.791 m)
Barrel Length	16 ft, 2 in (196 mm) / L56 (56 calibers)
Height	6 ft, 11 in (2.10 m)
Caliber	3.46 in (88 mm)
Barrels	One
Breech	Horizontal semiautomatic sliding block
Recoil	Independent liquid and hydropneumatic
Carriage	Sonderanhanger 202
Elevation	-3 to +85
Traverse	360 degrees
Maximum Firing Range	32,500 ft (9900 m) maximum ceiling

Muzzle Velocity: 2,690 ft/s (840 m/s)

Effective Firing Range: 16,250 yds (14,860 m) ground target, 26,240 ft (8000 m) effective ceiling

Sights: ZF.20

Rate of Fire: 15–20 rpm

VENGEANCE WEAPONS

Unconfirmed reports of German weapon development programs abound. Among the most disturbing of these, currently rumored to be in the testing and development phase, is the "vengeance weapon" program.

The *vergeltungswaffen* or "vengeance weapons" are allegedly meant to be tools of retribution for Allied bombings against German cities. Our enemies have boasted of superweapons that will win the war for Germany, and these vengeance weapons are believed to be part of that program. These projects have reportedly undergone development in a top-secret Nazi facility on a secluded island in the Baltic Sea. Last year, Polish underground operatives provided information about the base and the weapons program to British intelligence. Intense

bombing by the Royal Air Force inflicted heavy damage but failed to destroy the site completely. *Time to go back.*

Allied intelligence summaries have provided indications that Germany is working on at least two missile types: limited-range munitions with a gyrocompass autopilot, and a long-range ballistic munition. Although the technical name for the long-range missile is the Aggregat 4 or A4, rumors have circulated that the munitions may be designated V-1 and V-2 (Vengeance 1 and Vengeance 2).

Several launch sites for the limited-range munitions have already been built along the French coast. Allied bombings have thus far only been partially successful in neutralizing these sites. It is speculated that the V-1 will utilize a pulsejet engine and autopilot system

What the hell's that?

Movie people can't even make this stuff up.

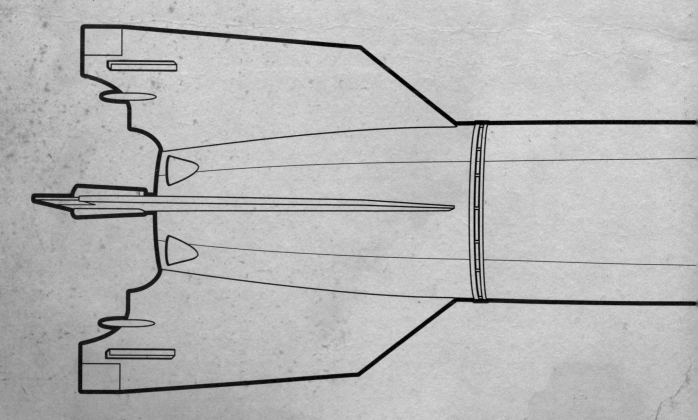

The following specifications are unknown or unavailable.

SPECIFICATIONS: V-1	
Class	Limited-range guided missile
Weight	UNKNOWN
Length	UNKNOWN
Width	UNKNOWN
Height	UNKNOWN
Warhead	UNKNOWN
Warhead Weight	UNKNOWN
Engine	UNKNOWN
Speed	UNKNOWN
Guidance System	UNKNOWN
Operational Range	UNKNOWN

SPECIFICATIONS: V-2 or A4	
Class	Single-stage ballistic missile
Weight	UNKNOWN
Length	UNKNOWN
Diameter	UNKNOWN
Warhead	UNKNOWN
Detonation Mechanism	UNKNOWN
Speed	UNKNOWN
Guidance System	UNKNOWN
Operational Range	UNKNOWN

and will be capable of delivering an amatol (TNT–ammonium nitrate mixture) warhead against an area target.

Thus far, we anticipate that our greatest defense against the V-1 will be antiaircraft guns. More effective countermeasures, however, are currently in development.

A Polish underground report of a "monstrous torpedo" and further evidence gathered from

fallen, unexploded test rockets point to the A4 being capable of carrying 1 ton of high explosives for 200 miles at a speed that could make it effectively invisible.

No launch sites for the A4 are known at this time, and none have been used against the Allies yet, but it appears to be only a matter of time. As of now, it is unknown when and where those weapons of terror might strike.

Don't sugarcoat it, I'm a big boy.

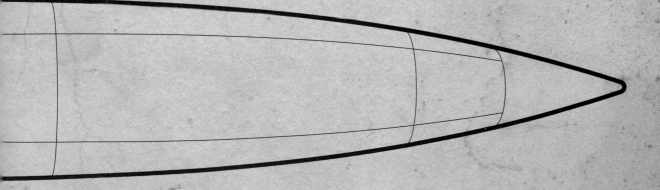

ANTITANK OBSTACLES

Mountains, cliffs, oceans .

Antitank obstacles can come in many forms. Mines, such as the German Teller mine, have proven brutally effective. While earlier mines would only damage tank treads, modifications to German antitank land mines have resulted in variants that can kill an entire crew.

In addition to mines, antitank obstacles that may be encountered include dragon's teeth and Czech hedgehogs. Dragon's teeth are pyramid-shaped obstacles made of reinforced concrete, two to three feet tall. Their purpose is to divert tanks into preregistered linear fire zones. Mines, steel beams, and barbed wire are also sometimes placed between them as a further hindrance. Specialized engineering vehicles can be called in to clear these obstacles.

I woulda called 'em porcupines.

Czech hedgehogs are so named because of their Czechoslovakian origins. They are mostly made from steel or wood such as railroad ties. In the case of metal, three pieces are joined by plates, rivets, and bolts (or simply welded together) in the shape of a three-armed cross. "Feet" on the arms are meant to prevent them from sinking in sand or mud, and some have notches for barbed wire. The obstructions are typically mounted in a poured concrete base, which makes them extraordinarily difficult to remove. They are effective even if tipped over or rolled and are able to withstand 60 metric tons of force. The most effective way to overcome hedgehogs is to use demolitions or blast them.

Wait . . . yeah. Yeah I get it!

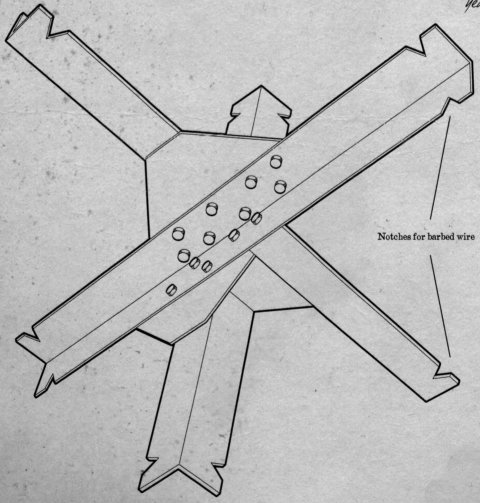

Notches for barbed wire

Dearest Red,

I can't imagine what you're going through, but I know you can handle anything they throw at you.

I looked in on your Pa yesterday; he was out there working even harder than usual. I suspect all that hard work is his way of dealing with you being gone.

My family's holding up. We keep our lights off at night, and none of us drive much due to the gas rationing. We all just want to do our part. I still work the grocery five days a week, plus helping Mom and Dad on the farm. Money's tight, but I managed to buy a war bond. Fifty bucks! It takes a bit from what I've been saving for college, but that's okay. You know once I set my mind to something I don't give up.

I miss you every day. I miss our picnics out by the old oak tree, where we'd wait for the sky to grow dark and watch the stars come out.

We have so much to do when you get home, but right now all I want you to worry about is keeping safe. Just know that there are happier times ahead and that we're here for you. Know that I love you and miss you and that I'm counting the days until your return.

Love,
Hazel

WAR MACHINES

The Vehicles of War

INTRODUCTION

In war, aircraft, vessels, and vehicles all have a specific purpose, whether it is to destroy the enemy, deliver supplies, or transport wounded personnel.

Extensive testing is conducted. Prototypes are created. As these machines are put to use in battlefield conditions, however, opportunities for improvement become clear. Changes are made, modifications are added, and in cases where superiority is gained, enemy designers quickly move to counter with their own upgrades.

The various machines in use by the Allies are being built swiftly and on a massive scale. They must all stand up to the rigors of combat and be operational in extreme weather conditions and over the most formidable terrain our planet has to offer.

Many of these ships, aircraft, and vehicles have already built outstanding reputations and gained the trust and <u>devotion</u> of their operators. Some have gained a kind of celebrity status, and others are surely destined to become legends with the passing of time.

For the individual service member, knowledge of both Allied and Axis vehicles is critical. Combat situations may force a soldier to operate an enemy vehicle.

The following is a list of notable aircraft, naval vessels, and vehicles, along with comprehensive information and specifications.

That's putting it gently.

Comfort's not a concern? Unbelievable!

Not too much devotion, I hope.

LCVP/HIGGINS BOAT

The Landing Craft, Vehicle, Personnel (LCVP), also commonly known as a Higgins boat after its designer Andrew Higgins, is a craft meant for amphibious landings. The boat was modeled after craft used in swamps and marshes and was originally intended for trappers and oil drillers. The LCVP is capable of operating in 18 inches of water and can accommodate thirty-six troops.

The most common method of entering the craft is from a cargo net suspended on the side of troop transport. The preferred method of exiting the craft, especially in an amphibious landing, is via the bow ramp.

When the United States Marine Corps first expressed interest in Higgins's boats, the bow ramp was not a feature. Higgins's first attempt, the LCP(L) (Landing Craft, Personnel, Large) forced troops to disembark over the sides, exposing men to enemy fire. Looking for a solution, Higgins studied Japanese bow-ramped boats. His revamped design was the LCP(R), with the R standing for "ramped." Machine guns that had been positioned in the front

of the LCPL were separated further to each side to allow for troop movement. The biggest drawback of this new boat was the ramp size, which was too narrow and prevented soldiers from quickly disembarking.

Further design development of the Higgins LCP(L)/LCP(R) produced the LCVP—with the ramp the width of the boat, allowing for a full complement of troops to disembark as well as providing enough space to carry additional vehicles. The machine guns were relocated to the rear of the craft.

The top and sides of the LCVP are made of plywood and therefore provide minimal protection for the troops or vehicles inside. *You said it!* The lightweight and shallow draft make the LCVP capable of quickly depositing soldiers directly onto the beach and then returning to large ships in deep water.

Higgins boats have already seen wide use, proving particularly effective in North Africa, and will no doubt further prove their worth as the war continues to unfold.

unless the whole thing's getting shot to hell. Then you just get out any way you can.

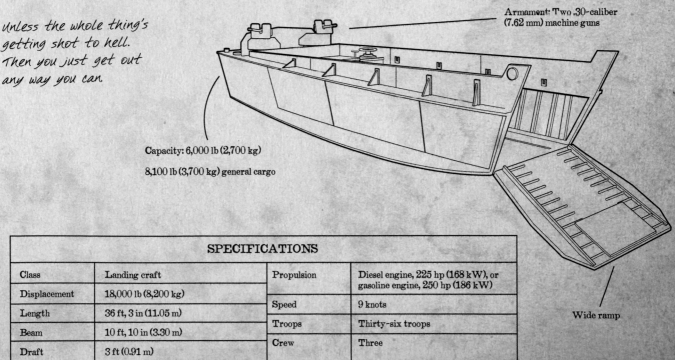

Armament: Two .30-caliber (7.62 mm) machine guns

Capacity: 6,000 lb (2,700 kg)

8,100 lb (3,700 kg) general cargo

Wide ramp

SPECIFICATIONS

Class	Landing craft	Propulsion	Diesel engine, 225 hp (168 kW), or gasoline engine, 250 hp (186 kW)
Displacement	18,000 lb (8,200 kg)		
Length	36 ft, 3 in (11.05 m)	Speed	9 knots
Beam	10 ft, 10 in (3.30 m)	Troops	Thirty-six troops
Draft	3 ft (0.91 m)	Crew	Three

USS SAMUEL CHASE (APA-26)

The *Samuel Chase* is an Arthur Middleton–class attack transport named after Samuel Chase, one of the signers of the Declaration of Independence. The Chase was built in Mississippi and originally launched under the name *African Meteor*. In February 1942, the Navy acquired the ship and commissioned it as the USS *Samuel Chase* (APA-26).

oh, THAT Samuel Chase.

The *Chase* is no stranger to the perils of battle. Since early 1942, she has amassed an incredible service record and miraculously avoided disaster on several occasions. During the Operation Torch amphibious landing in 1942, she survived days of repeated enemy attack by both bombs and torpedoes. The *Chase*'s survival is largely attributed to the crew's adept use of her .50 caliber antiaircraft machine guns. Thus effective use of the ship's defensive firepower earned her the nickname "Battleship" from our British allies. Operation Torch proved to be a turning point in the war, and the *Samuel Chase*'s involvement in its success cannot be overstated.

Don't jinx her!

Following Operation Torch, the *Samuel Chase* participated in the Invasion of Sicily, codenamed Operation Husky. The *Chase* did not lose a single soldier during this massive amphibious operation. As supplies piled up on the beach, the *Chase*'s crew made runs to unload the shift, aiding in yet another successful operation.

Who comes up with these?

Last year during Operation Avalanche, an amphibious landing in the Gulf of Salerno, two bombs came so close to striking the *Samuel Chase* that they tossed waves over the ship's bow. *Too close for comfort*

Now, after surviving numerous enemy threats and near misses, the USS *Samuel Chase* stands ready to charge boldly once more into the jaws of death.

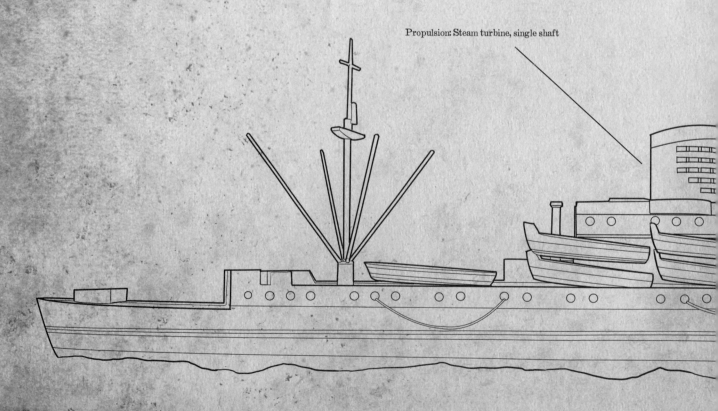

Propulsion: Steam turbine, single shaft

SPECIFICATIONS

Class	*Arthur Middleton*-class attack transport	Draft	27 ft, 4 in (8.33 m)
Displacement	11,760 tons	Speed	18.4 knots
Length	489 ft (149 m)	Complement	578 troops *You look stunning today.*
Beam	69 ft, 6 in (21.18 m)		

Armament: One 5-inch/38 dual-purpose gun mount

Four 3-inch/50 dual-purpose gun mounts

Eight .50-caliber AA machine guns

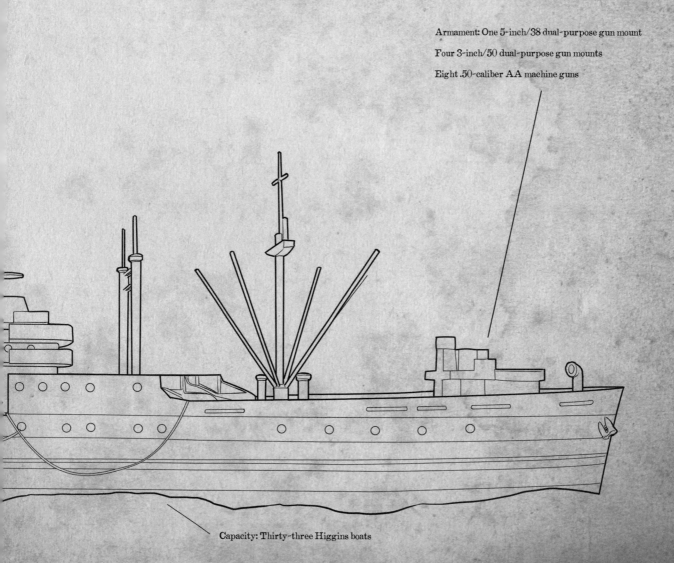

Capacity: Thirty-three Higgins boats

BENSON-LIVERMORE CLASS DESTROYERS

The intended purpose of destroyers began as fleet defense against torpedo boats. The name "torpedo-boat destroyer" was shortened to, simply, "destroyer."

The mission of destroyers soon expanded to include an antisubmarine role, as depth charges and sonar were added to the ship's inventory, and an antiaircraft role with the addition of antiaircraft guns. Destroyers now act as screening vessels against attack on larger warships, escorts for merchant ships, and sometimes as scouts for battle fleets.

In recent years, new classes of destroyers have emerged. Following the Great War, treaty restrictions enforced a 1,500 long ton limit on standard displacement, and ships built during this time were referred to as "1,500 tonners." Under the Second London Naval Treaty of 1936, tonnage limits were lifted, and the new class built during this time was the *Sims*, which added 70 tons.

Benson class destroyers were built on the same hull as the Sims. A subclass, *Livermore*, was created when differences in the complexity of the machinery on board emerged. *Benson* utilized less complex single-reduction gears and no cruising turbines. *Livermore* kept the more complex machinery and was named after the first ship, *USS Livermore*, to feature it. Together these ships comprise the *Benson-Livermore* class.

The greatest innovation to come from this class of destroyers is its "echeloned," or two-unit, machinery arrangement, where each unit contains its own fireroom, stack, and engine room. With this feature, a torpedo hit will not cripple the ship's propulsion system.

The *Benson-Livermore* class of destroyers has participated in every major campaign of the war and continues to challenge long-held notions of what the destroyer class of ships is capable of.

Basically says everything you need to know

Is there anything it doesn't do? Do we even need other ships?

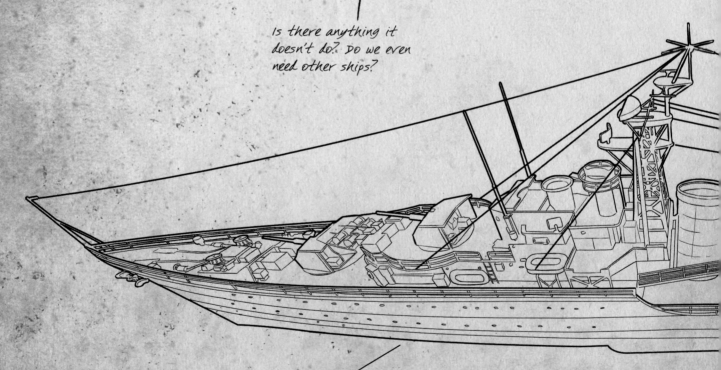

Four boilers

SPECIFICATIONS: *BENSON*-CLASS DESTROYER

Displacement	1,620 tons	Propulsion	Two shafts
Length	348 ft (106 m) overall; 341 ft (103.9 m) waterline	Speed	36.5 kn (67.6 km/h); 33 kn (61.1 kh/h) full load
Beam	36 ft (10.97 m)	Range	5,580 nmi (10,334 km, 7,500 mi) at 12 kn
Draft	11 ft 9 in (3.58 m) normal; 17 ft 9 in (5.41 m) full load	Complement	276

Armament: Five 5-inch (127 mm) dual-purpose guns

Ten .50-inch (12.7 mm) antiaircraft machine guns

One 21-inch quintuple torpedo tube

Six geared steam turbines

USS ARKANSAS

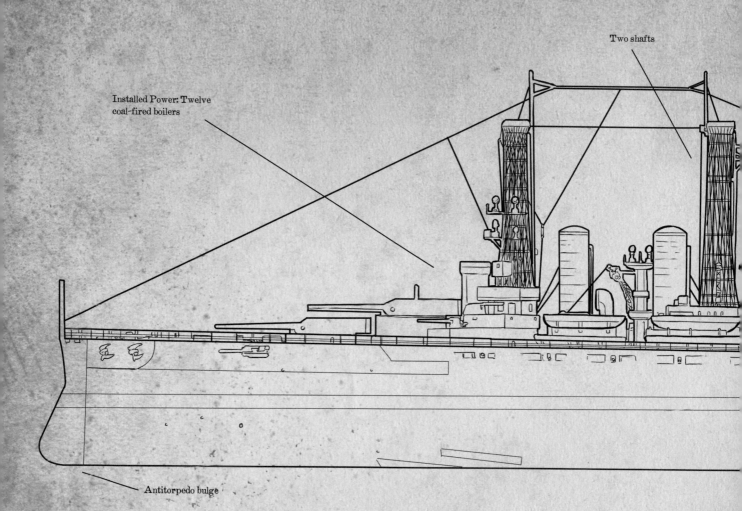

Two shafts

Installed Power: Twelve
coal-fired boilers

Antitorpedo bulge

Numerous types of warships exist on both the Allied and Axis sides. Fleet warships—warships that function as part of a battle fleet—consist of aircraft carriers, battleships, battlecruisers, pocket battleships, cruisers, and destroyers.

There's GOTTA be a story there.

In the simplest terms, a battleship is a large, relatively slow warship with thick armor and heavy-caliber guns (for comparison, a battlecruiser possesses less armor but is faster).

The HMS *Dreadnought* was introduced by the United Kingdom's Royal Navy in 1906 and redefined ship building by boasting more heavy-caliber guns than previous ships and utilizing steam turbine propulsion for greater speed—features that were revolutionary at the time. The resulting worldwide arms race led to vast improvements and technological advances that in turn led to the even more powerful super-dreadnoughts.

The Royal Navy's dreadnoughts proved to be of central importance in the Great War, as demonstrated by the successful naval blockade of Germany. In the years following the Great War, many naval treaties placed restrictions on the number and size of battleships serving in a particular nation's navy.

With the advent of aircraft and aircraft carriers, the role of battleships has and

I'm sure Germany "worked around" 'em.

SPECIFICATIONS

Class	Wyoming-class battleship	Speed	21.05 kn (38.98 kh/h, 24.22 mph)
Displacement	27,243 tons	Range	8,000 nmi (15,000 km, 9,200 mi) at 10 kn (19 km/h, 12 mph)
Length	562 ft (171 m) overall		
Beam	93 ft, 1 in (28.37 m)	Complement	1,036
Draft	28 ft, 6 in (8.69 m)	Armament	Twelve 12-inch guns, twenty-one 5-inch guns, two 21-inch torpedo tubes

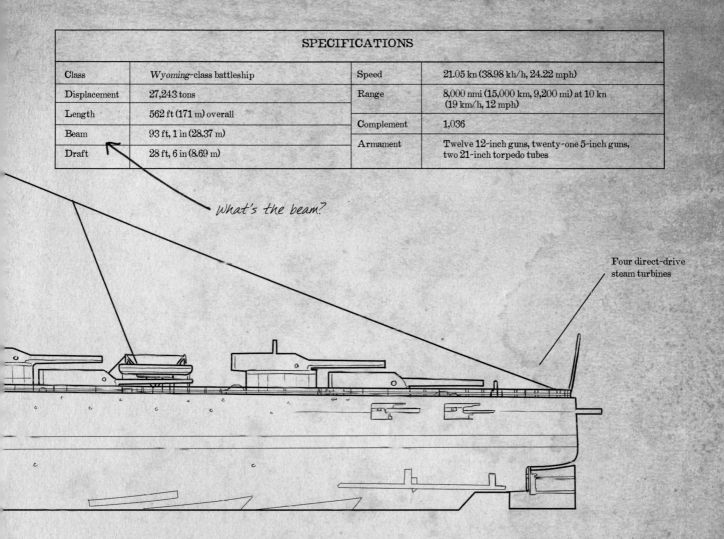

What's the beam?

Four direct-drive steam turbines

will continue to evolve to include providing defense against air attacks while escorting carriers, or bombarding shore defenses during amphibious landings.

The *Wyoming* class of battleship was developed in the US as a result of improvements made during the arms race and consists of two battleships: the USS *Wyoming* and USS *Arkansas*, both built between 1910 and 1912. Improvements made to the *Wyoming* class from the preceding class include additional armament, resulting in twelve twelve-inch guns and greater armor, including a torpedo bulkhead.

Both ships reinforced the Royal Navy's Grand Fleet during the Great War and following the war received many upgrades to include antitorpedo bulges and antiaircraft guns.

The *Wyoming* was demilitarized as part of the London Naval Treaty of 1930 and has since become a training ship. The *Arkansas*, however, continues to serve proudly, most recently as an escort for convoys to North Africa.

Though her combat role has shifted, the USS *Arkansas* continues to stand defiant—a testament to power and ingenuity whose finest hour, perhaps, is yet to come.

I'm guessing you know something I don't.

P-47

The agile, swift, and tough-as-nails P-47 Thunderbolt—called "Jug" by pilots, which is short for "Juggernaut"—is a fighter and bomber.

The first prototype, designated XP-47B, was highly maneuverable despite its weight. The cockpit was described as "roomy and comfortable." The XP-47B was also fast, reaching top speeds of 440 miles per hour, powered by an eighteen-cylinder, 2,600 horsepower engine. As a ground attack bomber, the XP-47B could carry rockets or a bomb load of 2,500 pounds.

Well, put your feet up and pop a cold one.

Minor changes to the prototype XP-47B led to the military's adoption of the aircraft as the P-47B. In 1941 the USAAF ordered 171 of the new aircraft. Production went into overdrive, and over the course of manufacturing, changes and modifications continued, leading to numerous versions.

The most significant advance is found in the P-47D-15, which increases internal fuel capacity to 370 gallons and provides under-wing pylons for mounting external drop tanks. This major upgrade in fuel storage allows the P-47D-15 to serve as a much-needed fighter escort on bombing missions deep into German territory.

"Borrowed" Most recently, the P-47D-25 has added a bubble canopy, adapted from a British feature created for their Hawker Tempest. The bubble allows the pilot a maximum unobstructed field of view, particularly for the crucial 6 o'clock position.

In aerial combat, the P-47 has proven capable of outmaneuvering enemy aircraft through rolls, climbs, and especially dives. The P-47 is the fastest-diving aircraft currently known to exist, reaching speeds of 550 miles per hour.

The P-47 is armed with eight AN/M2 .50-caliber machine guns. These weapons make the aircraft an effective platform for aerial combat as well as a workhorse of tactical close air support missions against ground targets.

With all the accolades heaped upon the P-47, the greatest advantage of all has to be its ability to sustain considerable damage and still bring the pilot home.

I heard they can't climb for crap.

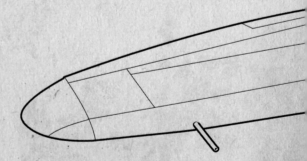

SPECIFICATIONS

Class	Fighter-bomber	Height	15 ft (4.57 m)
Empty Weight	10,000 lb (4535.92 kg)	Crew	One
Loaded Weight	19,400 lb (8,800 kg)	Range	1,800 mi (2896.82 km)
Length	36 ft (10.97 m)	Maximum Speed	426 mph (685.8 km/h)
Wingspan	40 ft 9 in (12.4 m)	Service Ceiling	40,000 ft (12,192 m)
Wing Area	300 sq ft (27.87 sq m)		

The plane is loaded and so am I!

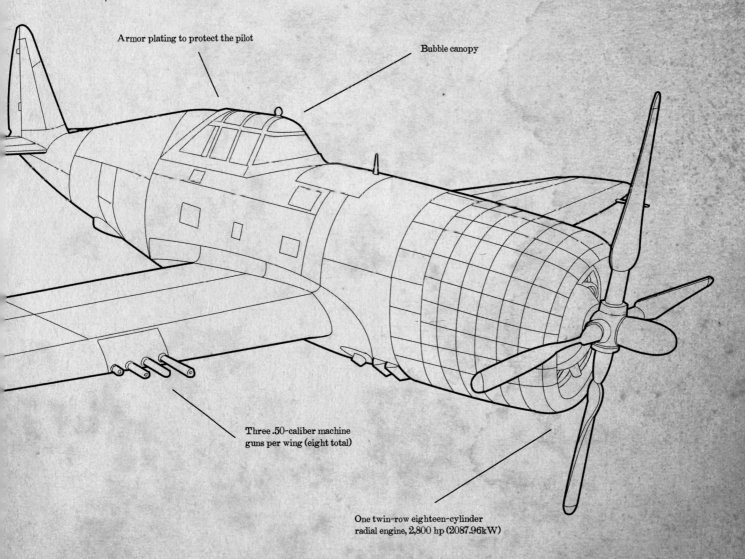

Armor plating to protect the pilot

Bubble canopy

Three .50-caliber machine guns per wing (eight total)

One twin-row eighteen-cylinder radial engine, 2,800 hp (2087.96kW)

M3 HALF-TRACK

Half-track designs (half-truck, half-tank) were pioneered by the British in the Great War. Though the concept soon fell out of favor, it experienced a resurgence in light of the Germans' effective use of the half-track as part of their "Blitzkrieg" tactics. It was a French design—the Citroën-Kégresse—that provided the inspiration for the vehicle that would ultimately become the M3 Half-track. The M2 was introduced as an artillery tractor but has since been adapted for many uses. The larger and longer M3 began production soon after the M2.

The body of the M3 is armored all around, including an armored radiator shutter and reinforced glass windscreen. Original M3s also feature a pintle-mounted .50-caliber machine gun, a feature that has been replaced in M3A1 models with the .50-caliber gun on an armored "pulpit mount," while .30-caliber machine guns can also be mounted on the sides of the passenger compartment. *Okay, I want one.*

The M3 has a single-access door in the rear and seating for twelve soldiers plus equipment, with five seats on each side in the rear and space for three in the cab. Beneath the seats are racks for ammunition and rations.

The use of commercially available parts whenever possible has guided the production philosophy of US half-tracks, not just for reliability but also for reasons relating to economy of scale. This has made it possible for dozens of variants to be made that are used for many purposes beyond simply "personnel carrier," including: casualty evacuation, equipment carrier, weapons platform, and light reconnaissance. Even with the mass production of the M3, demand for the half-track outpaced manufacturing early in the war (see M5 Half-track).

The M3 has come to be used on all major fronts and has cemented its role as a low-maintenance, all-terrain vehicle capable of getting the job done.

unless the job's in water. or the air. or underground...

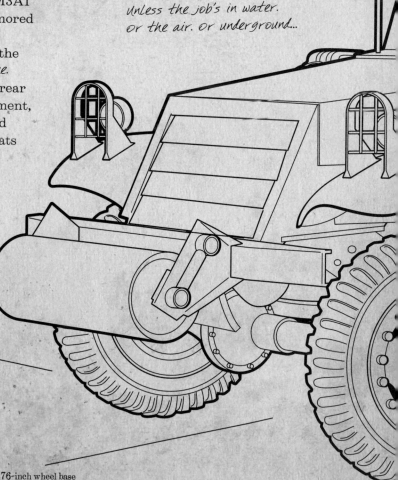

Front Suspension: Semielliptical longitudinal leaf spring

76-inch wheel base

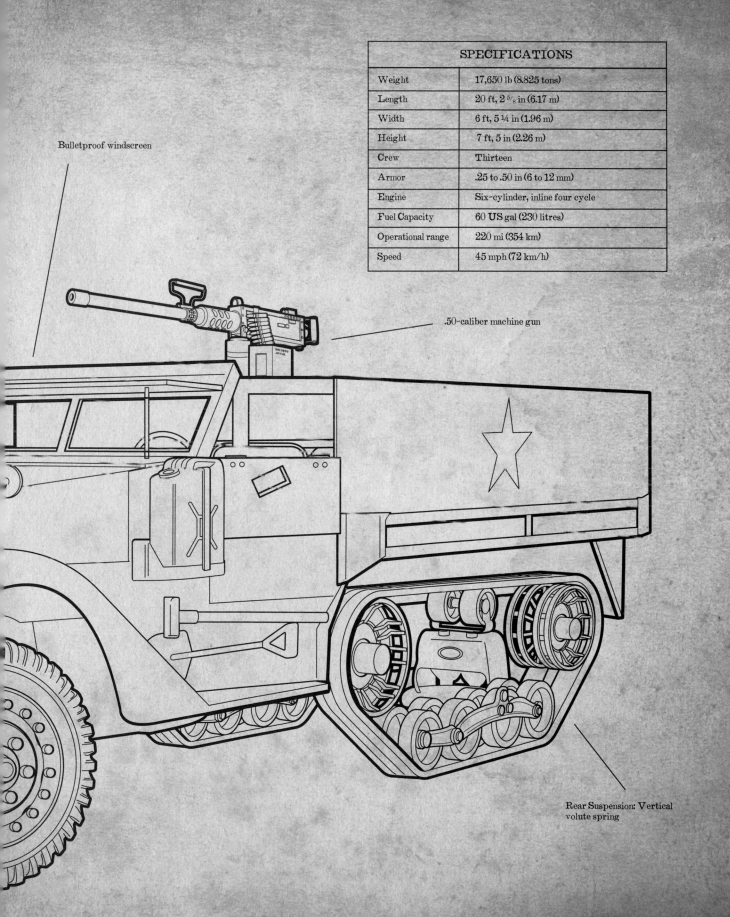

SPECIFICATIONS

Weight	17,650 lb (8.825 tons)
Length	20 ft, 2 $\frac{5}{8}$ in (6.17 m)
Width	6 ft, 5 $\frac{1}{4}$ in (1.96 m)
Height	7 ft, 5 in (2.26 m)
Crew	Thirteen
Armor	.25 to .50 in (6 to 12 mm)
Engine	Six-cylinder, inline four cycle
Fuel Capacity	60 US gal (230 litres)
Operational range	220 mi (354 km)
Speed	45 mph (72 km/h)

Bulletproof windscreen

.50-caliber machine gun

Rear Suspension: Vertical volute spring

M5 HALF-TRACK

The inability of manufacturers to keep up with the growing need for half-tracks (see M3 Half-track) in the early stages of the war led to the creation of the M5 Half-track. Given that the M5 is manufactured by a company using different equipment from what is used for the production of the M3, changes have been made to the design.

The M5 features rolled homogenous steel that is more vulnerable to armor-piercing rounds when compared to the face-hardened plate used on the M3. To counter this, the M5 mounts thicker armor, making the vehicle heavier. To accommodate the heavier weight, hull-strengthening components have been used, along with heavier axles.

As half-track demand has decreased, smaller numbers of M5s were ordered by the military until production stopped in October of last year. Under the Lend-Lease Act, M5s have been provided to allies of the United States. The British have used the M5 effectively as infantry transports, engineer vehicles, and command vehicles, and to tow six-pounder and seventeen-pounder antitank guns.

The M5A1 variant has a .50-caliber machine gun ring mounted over the assistant driver's side, plus a .30-caliber machine gun socket mount on both sides and at the back of the passenger compartment.

Decrease in half-track demand notwithstanding, the M5 has proven to be just as rugged and dependable as its M3 counterpart.

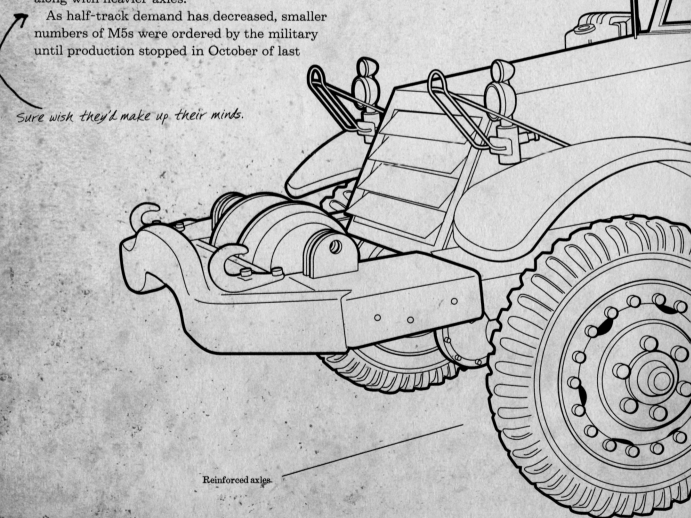

Reinforced axles

SPECIFICATIONS

Weight	18,425 lb (9.2 t)	Engine	Six-cylinder, inline, four cycle
Length	20.8 ft (6.3 m)	Power/weigh	16.2 HP/metric ton
Width	7.3 ft (2.23 m)	Fuel Capacity	60 US gal (230 liters)
Height	9 ft (2.74 m) overall	Operational range	220 mi (254 km)
Crew	Thirteen	Speed	42 mph (68 km/h)
Armor	3.11-.62 in (79-15.8 mm)		

Main Armament: One .30- caliber machine gun

Secondary Armament: 1.45-caliber submachine gun

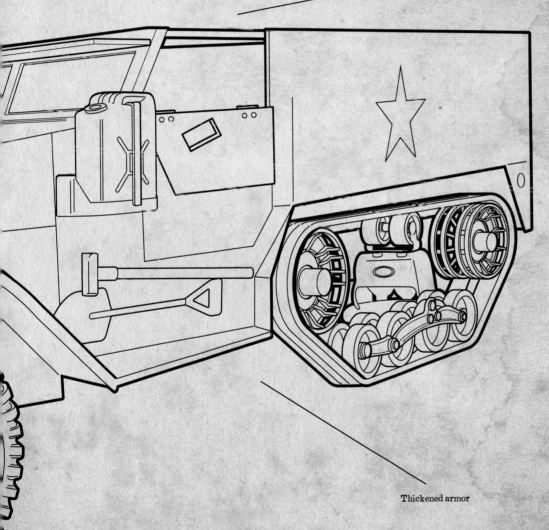

Thickened armor

M4 SHERMAN

The medium tank M4, or the M4 Sherman, is one of the most widely produced and utilized tanks in this war. It is employed not only by the United States, but also by the Commonwealth and the Soviet Union through the Lend-Lease program. It was the British who named the tank after the Civil War general William Tecumseh Sherman.

The ubiquity of the M4 is attributed to not only its reliability, but also the fact that it is relatively inexpensive and easy to manufacture.

Following improvements to the M3 medium tank design, a prototype designated the T6 was built and tested. The T6 retained the engine, transmission, tracks, and suspension system of the M3, but it reduced the crew from six to five, increased armor (but not at the cost of weight), and most important, placed the 75-mm main gun on a fully traversing turret (the M3's 75-mm gun was mounted in a limited-traverse turret, which meant that the

The name "Custer" didn't make the cut.

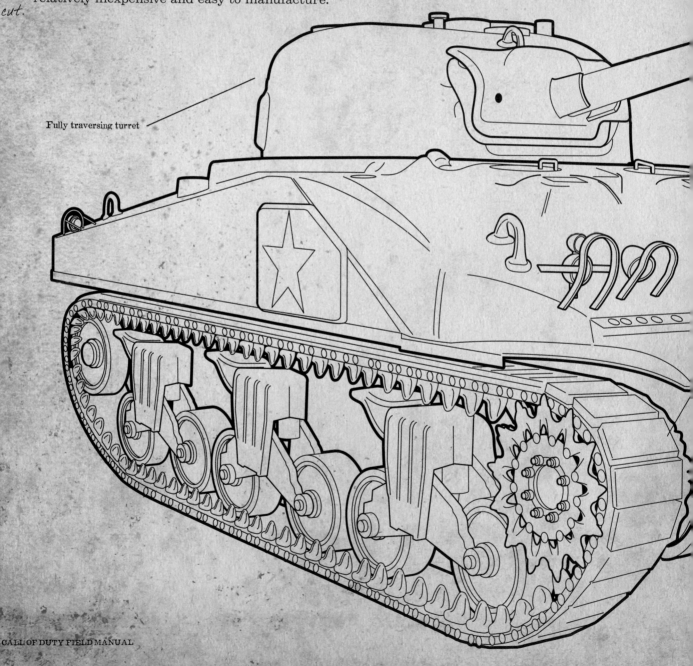

Fully traversing turret

SPECIFICATIONS: M4	
Weigh	33 tons (29,937 kg)
Length	19.16 ft (5.84 m)
Width	8.6 ft (2.62 m)
Height	8.99 ft (2.74 m)
Crew	Five
Engine	Continental R975 C1 nine-cylinder gasoline-fueled engine
Range	150 mi (240 km)
Speed	24 mph (38.5 km/h)

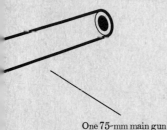

One 75-mm main gun

One .30-caliber machine gun

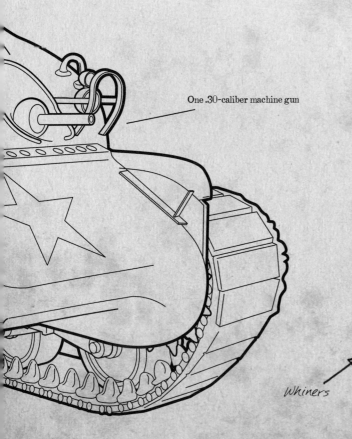

Whiners

entire tank was sometimes forced to turn in order to fire on the enemy). The 75-mm M3 is a long gun capable of penetrating 3.4 inches of <u>unsloped</u> armor at 110 yards (100 m), firing an M61 shell. Canister shots may be employed as well and can effectively function as giant shotguns. Also noteworthy is the 75 mm's use of a <u>gyroscopically</u> stabilized gun and sight, capable of retaining the gun's elevation setting within one-eighth of a degree through <u>mildly rough terrain</u> at 15 miles per hour.

"Hang on, we'll be right with you!"

That's a fake word

you know, a few rocks

The prototype T6 underwent design development and was subsequently standardized as prototype, which soon resulted in the M4, which began production in 1942. Though the original intention was to use M4s primarily in striking enemy rear positions, the realities of the current conflict soon made it clear that the greatest use of the Sherman would be in an infantry support and tank-versus-tank capacity.

The five-man crew of an M4 consists of the driver, <u>assistant driver/bow gunner</u>, ammunition loader, gunner, and tank commander.

Does he get twice the pay?

Several variants of the M4 exist, with the majority of differences being in the engine. Other notable variations include a cast versus a welded hull for the M4A1, and diesel engines instead of gasoline for the M4A2 and M4A6. Improvements have been made to all versions throughout the war, and design development continues. Enemy improvements in tank firepower and armor led the United States to begin the development of a heavier main gun, the 76 mm, which is currently in production. Also in production is a British variant of the M4—the Sherman Firefly—that mounts a 3-inch (76.2 mm) caliber British seventeen-pounder antitank gun in place of the 75 mm. Several other vehicles, including amphibious and recovery tanks, use the M4 chassis or hull.

Among the criticisms leveled at the Sherman are crew complaints of ammunition fires following a direct hit and the tank's inability to turn in place.

Despite any shortcomings, the M4 Sherman remains the United States' swiftest, most dependable, and most effective battle tank.

SD.KFZ. 10

US soldiers must be able to recognize these enemy vehicles should they spot them on the battlefield.

Light half-tracks like the Sd.Kfz. 10 fill a number of roles in the German army. The primary function of the Sd.Kfz. 10 is to haul or tow heavy or crew-served weapons such as antiaircraft guns, infantry support guns, and antitank guns. The Sd.Kfz. 10 is capable of transporting eight troops as a light armored personnel carrier in addition to towing a gun or trailer.

The Sd.Kfz. 10 is one of the most widely used German vehicles currently in service. Its designation comes from the name *Sonderkraftfahrzeug,* or special motorized vehicle. The chassis for the enemy vehicle Sd.Kfz. 251 (also referenced in this manual) was based on the Sd.Kfz. 10.

The Sd.Kfz. 10's design differs from other German half-tracks in that it uses a hull and not a frame. Should circumstances call for a US soldier to operate an Sd.Kfz. 10, be aware that the vehicle uses a semiautomatic transmission with seven forward and three reverse gears. Once a gear is chosen, the driver will need to depress the clutch to shift. For steering, a light turn uses just the front wheels, while harder turns will brake the tracks. Top speed is close to 50 miles per hour. Note that as with any continuous-tracked vehicle, disabling the tracks will immobilize it.

SPECIFICATIONS	
Weight	10,800 lb (4,900 kg)
Length:	15.6 ft (4.75 m)
Width	6.3 ft (1.93 m)
Height	6.6 ft (2 m)
Crew	Eight
Engine	Six-cylinder, water-cooled, 100 horsepower
Ground Clearance:	13 in (32 cm)
Fuel Capacity	29 gal (110 liters)
Operational range	190 mi (300 km) (road)
Speed	47 mph (75 km/h) (road)

Several variants of the Sd.Kfz. 10 exist: The Sd.Kfz. 10/1 is a chemical detection vehicle, used in transporting poison gas detection groups and/or to tow mortars or rocket launchers capable of delivering poison gas and smoke shells. The Sd.Kfz. 10/2 is a chemical decontamination vehicle capable of hauling eight 110-pound barrels of decontamination chemicals and fitted with a spreader. The Sd.Kfz. 10/3 is built to haul a 130-gallon tank used to spray poison gas. The same vehicle has been reported to utilize rocket launchers and antitank guns. The Sd.Kfz. 10/4 and 10/5 incorporate mounts for Flak 30 (and recently Flak 38) antiaircraft guns, are capable of transporting the seven-man crew, and generally tow an ammunition trailer. Last year these variants began appearing with armor plating.

Just call it "half-track 10" and save me a headache!

This is like when you play a record backwards.

Not bad for a vehicle that can't decide if it's a tank or a truck.

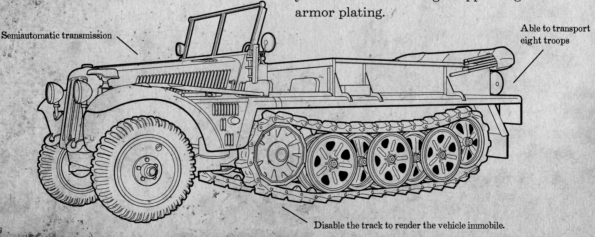

Semiautomatic transmission

Able to transport eight troops

Disable the track to render the vehicle immobile.

SD.KFZ. 251

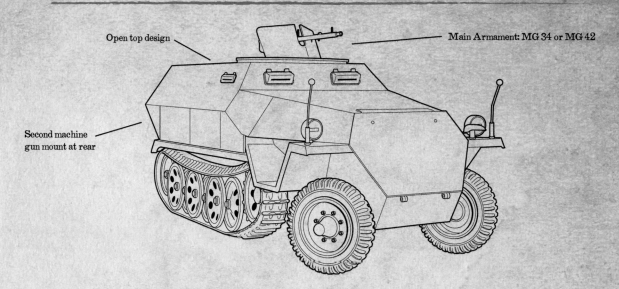

Open top design

Main Armament: MG 34 or MG 42

Second machine gun mount at rear

As with the Sd.Kfz. 10 referenced in this manual, it is necessary that a US soldier be aware of and be capable of recognizing the enemy Sd.Kfz. 251.

The Sd.Kfz. 251 is, like the Sd.Kfz. 10, a half-track vehicle. Unlike its counterpart, however, the Sd.Kfz. 251 is used primarily as an armored personnel carrier, a fighting vehicle meant to transport infantry into battle. Also known as "Hanomags" (named after the manufacturer), Sd.Kfz. 251s with their numerous variants are among the most abundant enemy vehicles seen in combat to date. A, B, C, and D main models of the half-track exist, and from those models several other variants have been observed.

The German army uses the Sd.Kfz. 251 primarily as an armored personnel carrier to protect up to ten soldiers (especially *panzergrenadiers*, or mechanized infantry) during transport and to provide covering fire while the troops dismount and engage in battle.

The standard weapon mount for a Sd.Kfz. 251 is an MG 34 or MG 42 machine gun at the front of the vehicle behind the driver. A second mount allows for another machine gun to be added to the rear. The vehicle's armor plating is capable of repelling rifle and machine gun fire. Armor thickness varies between 8 mm (side armor) and 14.5 mm (front armor).

Barrel aimed at his head

SPECIFICATIONS	
Weight	8.61 tons
Length	19 ft (5.80 m)
Width	6 ft, 10 in (2.10 m)
Height	5 ft, 9 in (1.75 m)
Crew	Twelve passengers
Engine	Six-cylinder gasoline
Power/weight	12.8 HP/metric ton
Suspension	Overlapping torsion bar (track), leaf spring (wheels)
Operational Range	186 mi (300 km)
Speed	32.5 mph (52.5 km/h)

These things are like rabbits.

Aside from the vulnerabilities inherent in any continuous-track vehicle, one feature of the Sd.Kfz. 251 that the Allies might exploit is the open-top design. Lack of overhead cover means that mortars, artillery fire, aircraft strafing, small arms fire from elevation, grenades, and even Molotov cocktails are all effective methods of attack.

Couldn't afford a roof?

Between the four main models, the biggest visual difference is in the D model, which features a single rear piece, flat doors, and less overall armor. There are numerous subvariants of the Sd.Kfz. 251, and while our intelligence is aware of fourteen different variants, it is likely that even more are in production.

SD.KFZ.6

Like other half-tracks used by the Wehrmacht, the Sd.Kfz. 6 is a German half-track military vehicle. It has not been encountered as widely as the Sd.Kfz. 10 or the Sd.Kfz. 251 and their variants. This is most likely because its primary function is as a tow vehicle for the 10.5 cm leFH 18 howitzer and also because it is heavier and more expensive to manufacture than the other vehicles.

Medium artillery tractor development dates back to the mid-1930s, when early designs were built by Bussing-NAG. Despite its designation as a medium-artillery tractor, Sd.KFz. 6 vehicles have been observed hauling much heavier loads than the type was designed to handle.

The Sd.Kfz. 6 is capable of transporting up to eleven soldiers in three rows and generally has a canvas cover. Reports on the engine vary, but intelligence suggests use of a NL38 six-cylinder engine at 90 horsepower, a later engine version with 100 horsepower, and potentially a Czech-built variant using a HL54 TUKRM, six-cylinder, 115 horsepower engine, giving the vehicle a speed of 31 miles per hour.

Known variants: The Sd.Kfz. 6/1 is capable of carrying fifteen soldiers and used to tow artillery. The Sd.Kfz. 6/2 is modified to transport the 37-mm Flak 36 antiaircraft gun. Ammunition for the gun is towed in a single-axle trailer. Though it is seen in much fewer numbers and thus far only in North Africa, the Sd. Kfz. 6/3 is noteworthy in that it features a superstructure designed to house the captured Soviet 76-mm divisional gun model 1936, a multipurpose field gun.

Could they have been a LITTLE more creative?

So what, did they get a ticket?

Those Krauts melt when they get wet.

Engine: Six-cylinder inline liquid cooled gasoline engine.

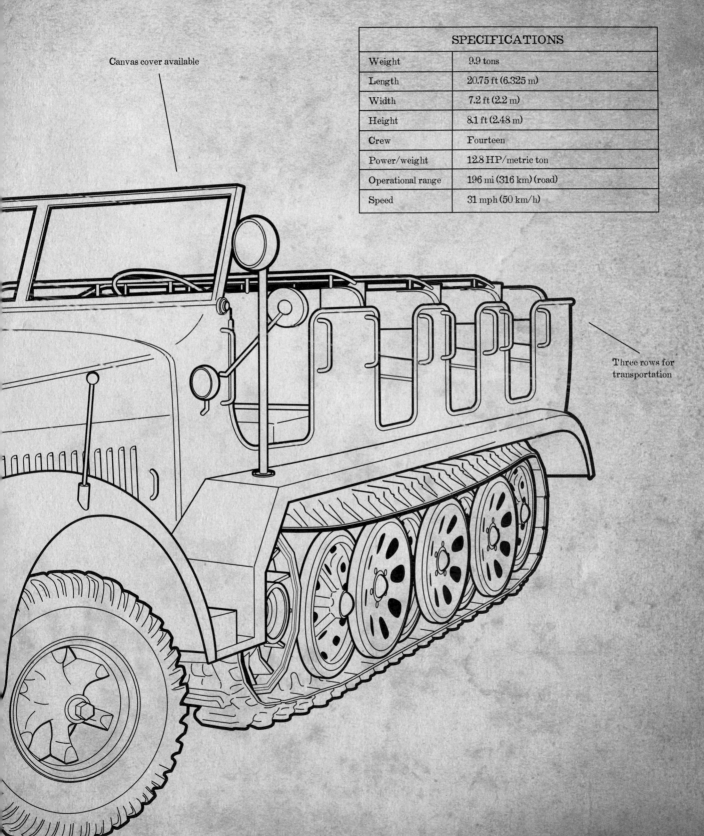

Canvas cover available

Three rows for transportation

SPECIFICATIONS

Weight	9.9 tons
Length	20.75 ft (6.325 m)
Width	7.2 ft (2.2 m)
Height	8.1 ft (2.48 m)
Crew	Fourteen
Power/weight	12.8 HP/metric ton
Operational range	196 mi (316 km) (road)
Speed	31 mph (50 km/h)

STURMGESCHÜTZ

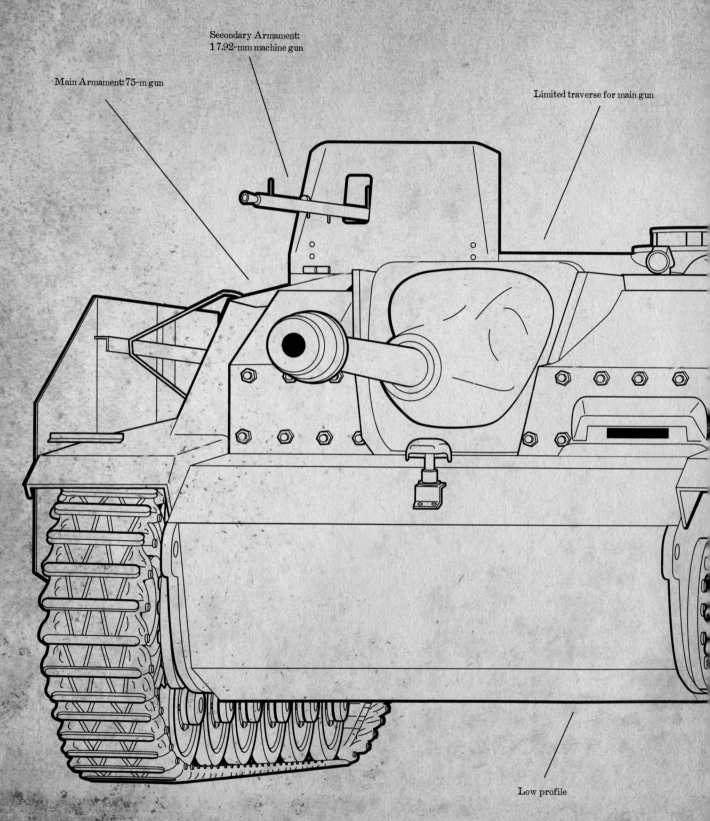

Secondary Armament:
17.92-mm machine gun

Main Armament: 75-m gun

Limited traverse for main gun

Low profile

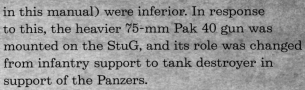

Our German enemies currently deploy the *Sturmgeschütz* ("assault gun"), an armored vehicle and mobile gun platform more commonly called the StuG.

The StuG was developed to provide the German military with a platform for mobile infantry support and antitank capability. Original prototypes were built on the Panzer III chassis and featured a 75-mm StuK 37L/24 gun that had limited traverse in a casemate-style hull.

Once the Germans went up against heavy Russian tanks like the T-34 and KV-1 during their invasion of the Soviet Union, they quickly discovered that their Panzers (also referenced in this manual) were inferior. In response to this, the heavier 75-mm Pak 40 gun was mounted on the StuG, and its role was changed from infantry support to tank destroyer in support of the Panzers.

The StuG still operates on a Panzer III chassis. It has no turret, but the vehicle's crew compartment proved sufficient to house the Pak 40 gun when the Panzers' turrets could not. The StuG's low profile makes it harder to detect and destroy. The main gun still has a limited traverse, however, making it necessary for the entire armored vehicle to turn in order to target the enemy. Additionally, early StuG versions had no light machine gun, making them vulnerable at close range. Many production models of the StuG (Ausf A-G) have since been produced, featuring various changes and improvements.

So all the other tanks make fun of it.

The RAF bombed the primary StuG manufacturer in November 1943, crippling production. To make up for the deficit, the enemy has begun mounting the StuG superstructure on a Panzer IV chassis. As a result, the original StuG is now called the StuG III, and this new variant is designated the StuG IV.

Makes WAY more sense than "StuG I"

SPECIFICATIONS: STUG IV	
Class	Assault gun
Weight	23 metric tons (50,705 lbs)
Length	20 ft (6.7 m)
Width	9 ft, 8 in (2.95 m)
Height	7 ft, 3 in (2.20 m)
Crew	Four
Armor	39-3.14 in (10-85 mm)
Engine	Twelve-cylinder
Range	130 mi (210 km)
Speed	25 mph (40 km/h)

GERMAN MAIN BATTLE TANKS

German tanks are officially designated *Panzerkampfwagen* ("armored combat vehicle"). It is necessary for US soldiers to understand the roles and capabilities of the enemy's rapidly growing armored branch.

Camp wagon?

The first Panzer was meant to be just a training tank. It is lightly armored and carries 2 7.92-mm MG13 machine guns. Despite its weaknesses, the tank was used effectively in the early stages of the war.

Drawing from the Panzer I design, the enemy created a larger version with a turret-mounted 20-mm antitank gun. Limited production models followed, improvements were made, and from those changes came the actual production models.

Many smoke breaks were taken.

The result was the Panzer II tank with a three-man crew capacity; 14 mm of armor on the sides, front, and back; and 10 mm on top and bottom. Armament is primarily a 2-cm KwK 30 L/55 autocannon with a 600 round-per-minute rate of fire. Additionally, the Panzer II uses a 7.92-mm MG34 machine gun.

While the Panzer II's main role was meant to be a reconnaissance tank, delays in Germany's production of heavier tanks meant that Panzer IIs entered combat service.

They ARE pretty stealthy.

Several variants of the Panzer II exist, including a version with remotely controlled flamethrowers. The Panzer II's chassis has also been used as a mount for heavy infantry and antitank guns. During the war's first campaigns, the Panzer II was the most widely used tank in the enemy arsenal, but in more recent years the Panzer II led to the development of the Panzer III and IV.

The Panzer III was developed to provide Germany with a clear advantage on the battlefield with a modern main battle tank that would serve a combat role against other tanks and armored vehicles. Medium and heavy Soviet tanks quickly made it necessary for the Panzer II to up-gun and up-armor, but Soviet tank designs still have the Panzer III at a disadvantage, forcing it into an infantry

Just don't get up-tight when we come after you.

support role. One noteworthy feature of the Panzer III is a three-man turret—providing for greater crew efficiency (by allowing each crewmember to focus on one task) and better situational awareness for the tank commander.

Like thumb-twiddlin'

The Panzer IV is the most widely used tank currently in German service. It is a medium tank used to combat other tanks like the Soviet KV-1 and T-34. To better combat other tanks, the Panzer IV was upgraded from its original 75-mm gun to the 75-mm KwK 40 L/43, capable of penetrating T-34 at ranges in excess of 3,000 feet.

Many production models of the Panzer IV exist, generally featuring upgrades in armor, guns, and engines. Also in keeping with previous Panzers, conversions using the Panzer IV chassis continue to enter service.

Together, the Panzer tanks present a formidable obstacle for our forces to overcome. This obstacle, however, is far from insurmountable, and the United States and her allies will not rest until the German war machine has ground to a halt.

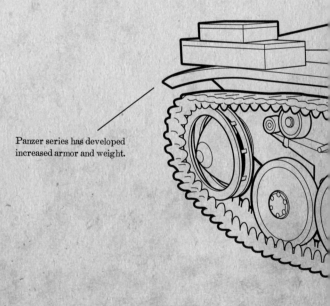

Panzer series has developed increased armor and weight.

SPECIFICATIONS: PANZER II

Class	Light tank	Armor	0.20-0.57 in (5-14.5 mm)
Weight	8.9 metric tons (8.8 long tons)	Power/Weight	15.7 PS (11.6 kW)/metric ton
Length	15 ft, 9 in (4.81 m)	Range	120 mi (200 km)
Width	7 ft, 3 in (2.22 m)	Speed	25 mph (40 km/h)
Height	6 ft, 6 in (1.99 m)	Main Armament	1 2-cm KwK 30
Crew	Three	Secondary Armament	1 7.92-mm Maschinengewehr 34

SPECIFICATIONS: PANZER III

Class	Medium tank	Engine	12-cylinder
Weight	20 tons	Range	103 mi (165 km)
Length	18 ft, 3 in (5.56 m)	Speed	25 mph (40 km/h) (road)
Width	9 ft, 6 in (2.90 m)	Armor	30-to 70-mm thick
Height	8 ft, 2 in (2.5 m)	Main Armament	One 37-mm gun; later versions: 50-mm gun
Crew	Five	Secondary Armament	Two 7.92-mm machine guns

PANZER II

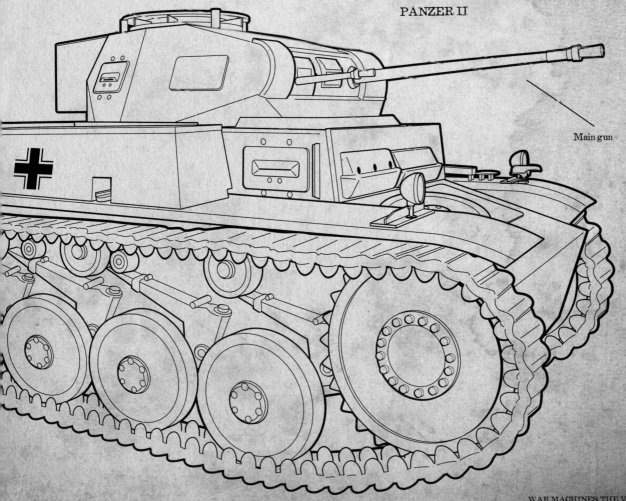

Main gun

PANZER IV

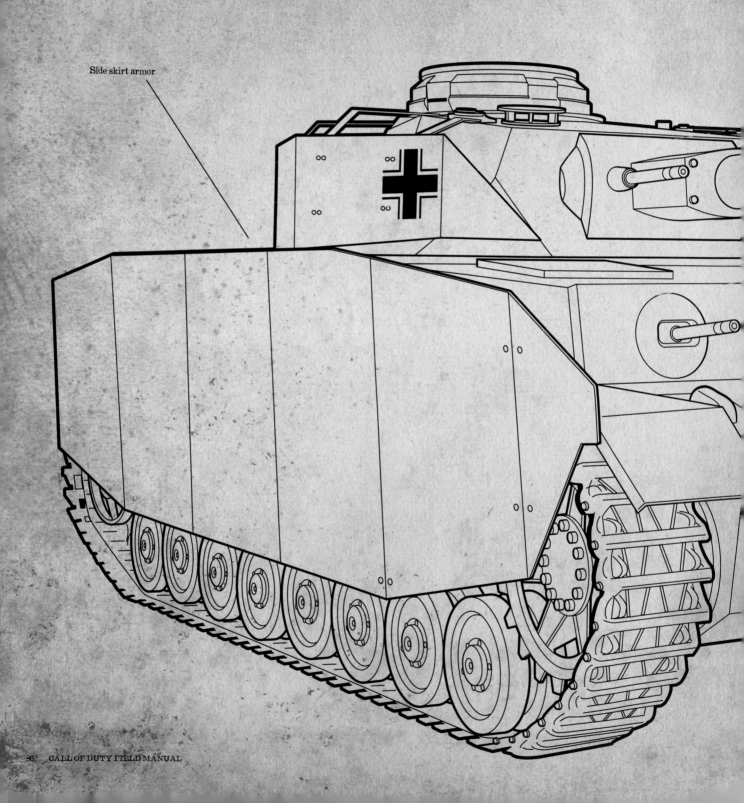

Side skirt armor

SPECIFICATIONS: PANZER IV

Class	Medium tank	Engine	Twelve-cylinder
Weight	25.0 tons	Range	120 mi (200 km)
Length	19 ft, 5 in (5.92 m)	Speed	26 mph (42 km/h) (road)
Width	9 ft, 5 in (2.88 m)	Armor	30 to 80 mm
Height	8 ft, 10 in (2.68 m)	Main Armament	One 75-mm gun
Crew	Five	Secondary Armament	Two 7.92-mm machine guns

Upgraded main gun with greater power

PANZERKAMPFWAGEN VI TIGER

"Tiger" is the nickname given to the enemy German heavy tank, Panzerkampfwagen VI Tiger Ausf E.

Following years of designs and prototypes for heavy tank models, the Tiger was chosen after modifications made in the wake of Operation Barbarossa, the invasion of the Soviet Union in 1941.

The Tiger operates with a five-man crew and features heavier armor, a bigger main gun, higher fuel and ammunition storage capacity, and a better engine, transmission, and suspension when compared to the Panzer IV (also referenced in this manual). Also noteworthy is that the Tiger uses a steering wheel rather than the usual tiller. It is capable of pivoting in place by turning the tracks in different directions. Its front hull armor is 3.9 in (100 mm) thick; the gun mantlet is 4.7 in (120 mm), the side plates 2.4 in (60 mm) and the turret sides and rear are 3.15 in (80 mm).

The front glacis of a Tiger can withstand direct fire from an M4 Sherman.

Too heavy for small bridges, the Tiger is capable of fording rivers, after time is taken to set up ventilation and cooling. Early models are capable of deep fording, while this feature was downgraded in later models.

The Tiger's main gun is a 56-caliber-long 8.8 cm KwK 36, chosen for its accuracy and penetration.

Throughout production, many revisions and changes have been made, and several production models have been developed. Early models are especially prone to breaking down, and freezing ice and snow can immobilize the Tiger.

The British variant of the Sherman, the Firefly, and the Soviet SU-152 have both proven capable of countering the Tiger. The US is currently in the process of up-gunning the Sherman tank to a 76 mm to take on the Tiger.

Over the last year, the Germans have worked to produce an upgraded version of the Tiger, the Tiger II. The Tiger II is rumored to utilize a sloping version of the Tiger I armor, is substantially heavier than its predecessor, and carries a long-barreled 8.8-cm KwK 43 L/71 antitank cannon.

While the Tiger II has not been seen in combat yet, it is surely only a matter of time until this latest version rolls onto the battlefield. As always, the United States and her allies must be ready to face this new enemy threat.

What the hell's a tiller? Doesn't that go on a boat?

What about indirect fire?

So many jokes

Crew: Five

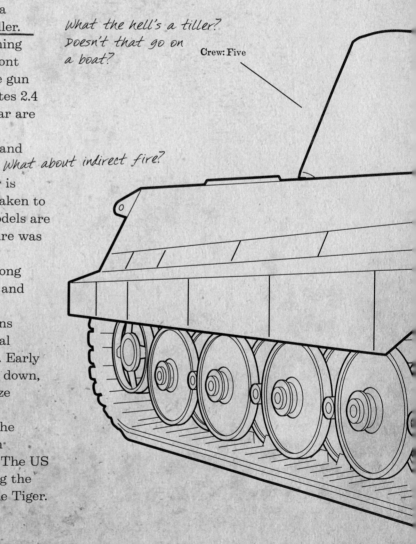

SPECIFICATIONS: TIGER I			
Class	Heavy tank	Engine	Twelve-cylinder
Weight	60 tons	Range	110 mi (170 km)
Length	20 ft, 9 in (6.3 m) hull	Speed	25.8 mph (42.5 km/h) (road)
Width	11 ft, 8 in (3.56 m)	Armor	60 to 100 mm thick
Height	9 ft, 10 in (3.0 m)	Main Armament	88-mm gun
Crew	Five	Secondary Armament	Two 7.92-mm MG 34 machine guns (5,850 rounds)

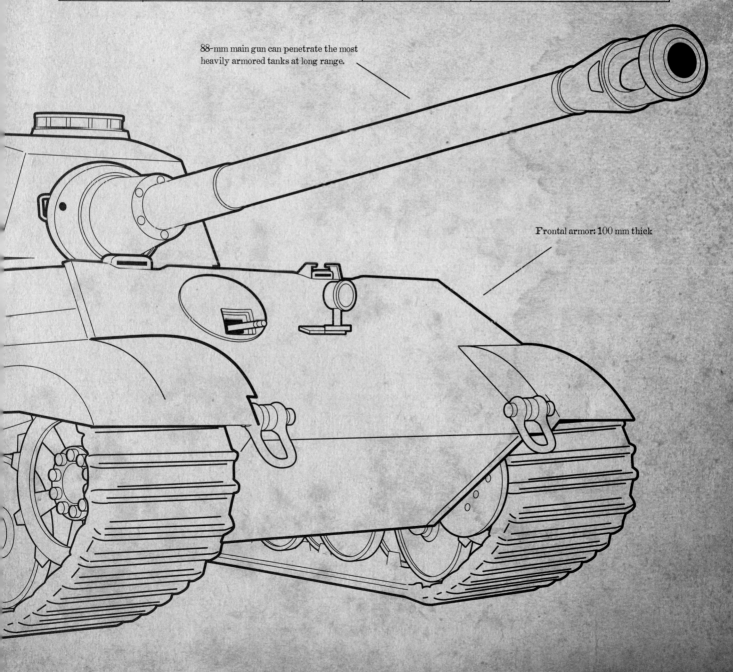

88-mm main gun can penetrate the most heavily armored tanks at long range.

Frontal armor: 100 mm thick

DEADLY GROUND

The Environments,
Locations, and
Terrain of War

INTRODUCTION

After an extensive air war, and with victory in the North African campaign and the subsequent invasion of Sicily last year, the Allies have sent an unmistakable message to the enemy: The war for Western Europe has begun.

As the focus of conflict shifts to northwestern Europe, new battlefield environments will be encountered. Lessons learned from previous engagements will provide invaluable insights, while advance knowledge of combat settings will allow for better strategic planning and greater chances of success.

No matter the setting, the same basic rules of combat apply: secure the area, gain and maintain the initiative, engage with and destroy the enemy, communicate effectively, and care for the wounded.

The following section lists possible terrain and settings that may be encountered, former operations that provide valuable lessons learned, and potential assault/Allied-advance scenarios.

That and, "You're about to get smoked!"

What's that one? I don't understand

Lesson 1: "Don't die"

Ah, the memories

THE ATLANTIC WALL

For years now the United States and Soviet Union have wanted to create a second front in Europe. With extensive campaigns waged in the Mediterranean theater of operations, with North Africa reclaimed from enemy hands, and with the Allied invasions of Sicily and Italy, there is an expectation on both sides that the Allies will once again look to open the long-desired second front.

It's about damn time!

Any attempted landings along the Atlantic Wall (the expansive coastline along continental Europe and Scandinavia defended by German forces) would surely face overwhelming opposition. In many cases, the geography itself presents a challenging hindrance. Add to this the fact that late last year, Field Marshal Erwin Rommel was tasked with strengthening German army forces along the French coast. Minefields, landing craft obstacles including

Misinformation. We obviously won't be landing THERE if they're talking about it in this manual.

For vampire defense.

wooden stakes, Czech hedgehogs, barbed wire, and bunkers are just some of the obstacles to take into consideration for any potential beach assault.

In Normandy alone, an Allied invasion force would be confronted with three to four infantry divisions with tank support and limited air support, numbering from 7,000 to 12,000 men each. All landing craft would need to be cautious of sandbars. Some landing forces would assuredly contend with sea walls and cliffs topped by gun batteries. With the aforementioned fortifications and obstructions meant to slow troop and vehicle movement, Allies on the wide-open coast would be exposed to withering enemy automatic weapons fire and artillery bombardment. An assault at high tide would mean less time spent in the water, but many of the obstacles placed under

Rommel's direction and leadership have been positioned at the high-water mark.

In the event of an Allied landing, those moving further inland would encounter terrain flooded by the Germans as well as mixed terrain of woodland and pasture, with fields hemmed in by ridges and banks and thick, entangling hedgerows. Soldiers would be forced to scale stone walls and wade through marshes, while close-quarter combat would be necessary in moving through towns and small villages, in order to clear houses and structures (see "Urban Warfare").

Throughout all of this, weather conditions would be a critical determining factor between victory and defeat.

Despite the myriad challenges, headway is already being made, as British and US air forces continue to drop supplies and weapons to resistance fighters, and to bombard the French rail network, making it difficult for the enemy to use those railways in the transport of troops and supplies.

Make no mistake: Freedom will prevail over tyranny; before this war is done, Allied forces will see northwestern Europe liberated from Nazi rule.

Just show me the way!

PARIS, FRANCE

It is no secret that liberating Paris is a primary Allied goal.

The German military has occupied Paris since June 14, 1940. Conditions for the citizens of Paris are deplorable. There is a curfew from 9 p.m. to 5 a.m., during which time blackout conditions are in effect. Restaurants serve noodles, beets, and turnips. Food, tobacco, coal, and clothing are all rationed, and French newspapers and radio only print and transmit German propaganda. Because of fuel shortages, there are almost no vehicles on the streets. Priceless works of art have been stolen by the Gestapo. Young Frenchmen have been pressed into service as factory workers. Third Reich flags fly, and clocks have been set to Berlin time.

That's torture enough right there.

It is no wonder that a million Parisians have fled the city. Most deplorable of all, thousands of Jews, including women and children, have been rounded up and sent to concentration camps. A French underground resistance exists, but they have been woefully outmatched, and since the occupation began, they have remained mostly silent. Their numbers, however, are growing. "V" for victory continues to appear on buildings and vehicles, and those willing to fight to retake their homeland have begun to rally.

Any efforts to liberate Paris will rely not on Allied action alone but rather on the desire and willingness of the people of Paris to rise up, to be willing to shed blood so that they might see the French flag fly over their beloved city once again.

The time is now! Send those Krauts packin'!

URBAN WARFARE

Operations within the theater of battle may include urban warfare as well as house and structure clearing in both small towns and villages and larger cities. In such cases, the following information could be crtical in saving your life.

Aerial photographs are critical and should be taken daily if possible.

Use tanks to eliminate outlying defenses, but don't let tanks and infantry become separated. Infantry should remain with tanks when entering a town or village to defend against enemy infantry.

Areas of operation should be assigned to each platoon or squad. Treat city blocks as a square. When one side of the square is secured, the right and left sides should be cleared next while a unit remains on the secured side, on the top floor, to fire into the back windows and doorways of enemy positions.

They get lonely.

Streets are deadly. Blow out locks of opposing doors, or destroy doors with M1 rocket launchers (referenced in this manual) before crossing a street. Use white phosphorous hand grenade smoke for concealment and cross quickly under covering fire. Clear ground floors first and use the M1 rifle (referenced in this manual) to fire through the floors above. If the enemy is in the basement, clear the area and use TNT to blow out the floor. Hallways, stairways, and rooftops may be used, but sometimes advancing units may be required to blow holes in the walls. In some cases, it may be necessary to burn the building. If so, do this at night.

Clear every room. Be thorough. You must not leave enemies behind the line to fire on Allies from behind.

Don't forget to yell "Knock knock!"

City blocks ARE a square.

FOREST FIGHTING

Basically forest fighting is scary as hell.

As with urban warfare, battling the enemy in a forest setting is a very real possibility. An Allied path to the ultimate objective—Germany itself, is likely to involve forest warfare. Forest regions such as the Grunewald, the Black Forest, Ardennes, and Hürtgen are found throughout the country.

An advancing army must take into account the consequences of fighting in such a setting. Vehicular movement through a forest like Hürtgen would be restricted due to the woods' density and lack of roads. Absence of open routes can make it difficult to deliver supplies and evacuate wounded soldiers. While the Hürtgen lacks roads, the Ardennes not only has pathways capable of accommodating transport, but it has already been used by the Germans to route mechanized forces for their invasion of France in one of the largest-scale armored movements ever carried out. The German Army cut through the Ardennes during the Battle of Dunkirk as well. Note that rivers such as the Moselle and the Meuse may also provide an obstacle that must be overcome.

I'm seeing a pattern here.

Advance knowledge of the specific forest to be entered is therefore key in any battle plan.

Invading forces moving through a forest must be vigilant against minefields, booby traps, barbed wire, and bunkers. Orientation within a forest setting can be difficult; battle lines can be vague. An especially thick canopy restricting sunlight, in addition to the numerous environmental opportunities for concealment, can make it difficult to be confident that the terrain has been cleared of enemy threats. Also, in the case of thick cover, air support cannot be relied on. Wooded terrain presents a problem for tanks while providing plenty of cover and concealment for antitank weaponry.

US soldiers should also be aware of the enemy's ability to use tree bursts. Proximity fuses can allow for the Germans to detonate artillery at the treetop level, which would send a deadly rain of shrapnel onto troops. While soldiers have been trained to hit the ground when artillery comes in, the best defense in a tree burst scenario is to hug the nearest tree.

With the above considerations taken into account, a military advance moving through wooded terrain will stand a much greater chance not only of survival but of success.

Save the trees!

You fight in one forest, you've fought in them all.

Snow! They didn't warn me about snow!

There's nothing like Christmas on the front lines, freezing with your platoon.

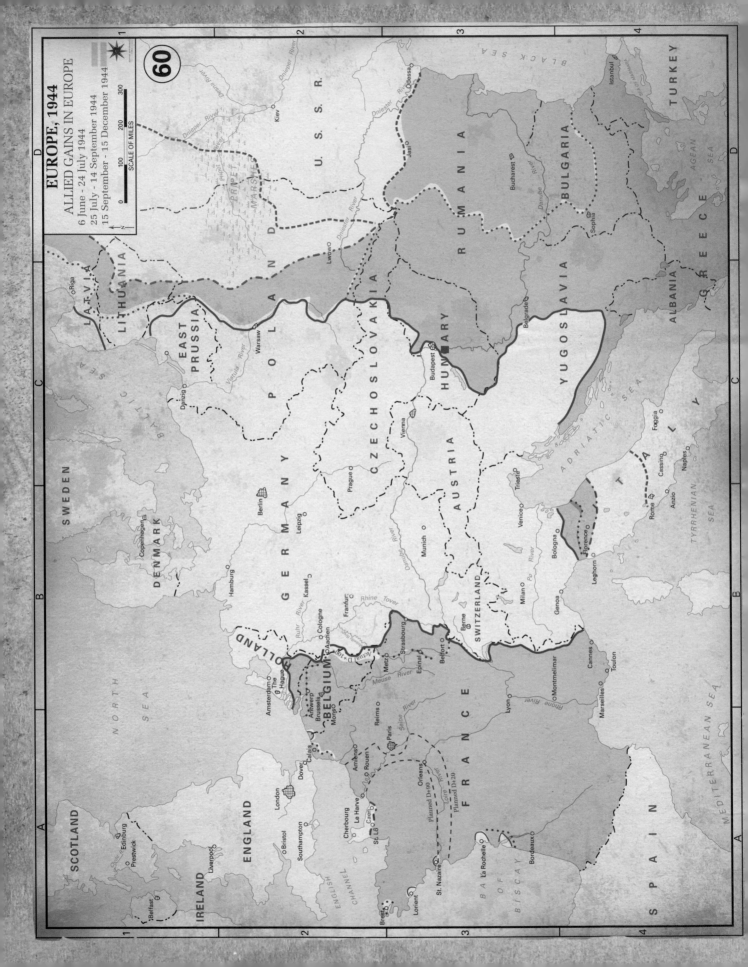

EUROPE, 1944
ALLIED GAINS IN EUROPE
6 June - 24 July 1944
25 July - 14 September 1944
15 September - 15 December 1944

SCALE OF MILES
0   100   200   300

SCOTLAND
Edinburgh
Prestwick

IRELAND
Belfast

Liverpool

ENGLAND
London
Bristol
Southampton

Dover
Calais
Cherbourg
Le Havre
Caen
St. Lô
Amiens
Rouen
Paris
Reims

ENGLISH CHANNEL

Brest
St. Nazaire
Lorient
La Rochelle
Bordeaux

Planned D-90
Planned D-20

Loire River

B A Y   O F   B I S C A Y

SPAIN

F R A N C E

Orleans
Seine River
Mons
Brussels
Antwerp
The Hague
Amsterdam

BELGIUM
HOLLAND

Lyon
Marseilles
Toulon
Cannes
Montmelimar
Rhone River

Metz
Epinal
Strasbourg
Belfort
Berne

SWITZERLAND

Aachen
Cologne
Frankfurt
Kassel
Hamburg

Rhine River
Ruhr River
Meuse River
Moselle
Tover

G E R M A N Y

Berlin
Leipzig

Copenhagen

DENMARK

SWEDEN

N O R T H   S E A

B A L T I C   S E A

Danzig

EAST PRUSSIA

P O L A N D

Warsaw
Vistula River

Riga

LATVIA
LITHUANIA

U. S. S. R.

Kiev
Dnieper River
Desna River
Pripet River

P R I P E T   M A R S H

Dniester River

Lwow

CZECHOSLOVAKIA

Prague
Vienna
Munich
Danube River

AUSTRIA

Budapest

HUNGARY

Trieste
Venice
Milan
Genoa
Po River
Bologna
Florence
Leghorn

I T A L Y

Rome
Anzio
Cassino
Naples
Foggia

A D R I A T I C   S E A

T Y R R H E N I A N   S E A

M E D I T E R R A N E A N   S E A

YUGOSLAVIA
Belgrade

RUMANIA
Bucharest
Jassy
Odessa
Danube River
Dniester River

BULGARIA
Sophia

BLACK SEA

GREECE
ALBANIA

AEGEAN SEA

TURKEY
Istanbul

Darling,

    Letters from home mean so much more than you could ever know. Sometimes that's all that keeps us going.

    I understand now why our division is called the Bloody First. I've faced death day after day, and the victories come at such a terrible price. I've seen too many good and brave men die.

    When I signed up, they called me "farmboy" and they were right—I was just a boy who thought he could take on the world. But that boy's gone now. I've seen too much.

    When I fight now, it's not because I've got something to prove. I fight so I can survive. So I can come home to you. To family.

    I think about you and the life that's waiting for me just about every minute of every day. I can't wait to see you. It won't be much longer now. It can't be.

I love you,
Red

TITAN BOOKS

A division of Titan Publishing Group Ltd
144 Southwark Street
London SE1 0UP
www.titanbooks.com

 Find us on Facebook: www.facebook.com/titanbooks

 Follow us on Twitter: @titanbooks

Published by Titan Books, London, in 2017.

Published by arrangement with Insight Editions, PO Box
3088, San Rafael, CA 94912, USA. www.insighteditions.com

A CIP catalogue record for this title is available from the
British Library.

ISBN: 9781785657511

Publisher: Raoul Goff
Associate Publisher: Vanessa Lopez
Art Director: Chrissy Kwasnik
Senior Designer: Stuart Smith
Senior Editor: Amanda Ng
Managing Editor: Alan Kaplan
Editorial Assistant: Maya Alpert
Production Editor: Elaine Ou
Production Managers: Alix Nicholaeff and Lina s Palma
Production Assistant: Jacob Frink
Written by Micky Neilson
Illustrations by Ian Moores and
Carlo Carlos Rafael Duarte/Watermark Rights

Additional text by Martin Morgan

Insight Editions, in association with Roots of Peace, will
plant two trees for each tree used in the manufacturing of
this book. Roots of Peace is an internationally renowned
humanitarian organization dedicated to eradicating land
mines worldwide and converting war-torn lands into
productive farms and wildlife habitats. Roots of Peace will
plant two million fruit and nut trees in Afghanistan and
provide farmers there with the skills and support necessary
for sustainable land use.

Manufactured in China

10 9 8 7 6 5 4 3 2 1

About the Author

Micky Neilson is a two-time *New York* Times best-selling
author whose graphic novels *Ashbringer* (#2 on the list)
and *Pearl of Pandaria* (#3) have both been published
in six languages. As one of the first writers at Blizzard
Entertainment, he has more than two decades of experience
in the cutting edge of the gaming industry. He is currently
working on a graphic novel, *Rook*, as well as a number of
film projects. In 2016, Riverdale Avenue Press published his
memoir, *Lost and Found: An Autobiography About Discovering
Family*. Most recently, he self-published his first full-length
horror novel, *The Turning*, and its sequel, *Whisper Lake*,
through Amazon.

Further Reading and Resources

American Rifleman,
https://www.americanrifleman.org/

D-Day Museum,
http://ddaymuseum.co.uk/

Guns & Ammo Magazine and Website,
http://www.gunsandammo.com/

HistoryNet,
http://www.historynet.com/

Naval History and Heritgae Command,
https://www.history.navy.mil/

The New Encyclopedia Britannica,
https://www.britannica.com

The Official Website of the United States Navy,
http://www.navy.mil/

Smithsonian National Air and Space Museum,
https://airandspace.si.edu/

United States Coast Guard Homepage. Accessed May 2017.
https://www.uscg.mil/

Additional source material for images

Page 4: *I want you for the U.S. Army* by James Montgomery
Flagg, 1917. Painting. Leslie-Judge Co., N.Y./Library of
Congress, Washington, D.C.

Page 110: Map courtesy of the USMA, Department of
History. Modified slightly from its original form.